SELECTED POEMS

OF

GERARD MANLEY HOPKINS

DOVER THRIFT EDITIONS

Edited and with an Introduction by
Bob Blaisdell

DOVER PUBLICATIONS, INC.
MINEOLA, NEW YORK

DOVER THRIFT EDITIONS

GENERAL EDITOR: MARY CAROLYN WALDREP
EDITOR OF THIS VOLUME: BOB BLAISDELL

Copyright

Bibliographical Note

This Dover edition, first published in 2011, is a new selection of poems from standard texts. A new introductory Note has been specially prepared for the present edition.

Library of Congress Cataloging-in-Publication Data

Hopkins, Gerard Manley, 1844–1889.
[Poems. Selections]
Selected poems of Gerard Manley Hopkins/Gerard Manley Hopkins;
edited and with an introduction by Bob Blaisdell.
p. cm.—(Dover thrift editions)
Includes bibliographical references and index.
ISBN-13: 978-0-486-47867-8
ISBN-10: 0-486-47867-X
I. Blaisdell, Robert. II. Title. III. Series.
PR4803.H44A6 2011
821'.8—dc22

2010048402

Manufactured in the United States by LSC Communications
47867X06   2018
www.doverpublications.com

Contents

Introduction

by Bob Blaisdell

~

Born on July 28, 1844, in Stratford, near London, Gerard Hopkins was the son of Manley Hopkins, an occasional writer whose profession was insuring ship-owners. Gerard (no one used his middle name Manley; that name became associated with the poet to distinguish him from another writer) was the eldest child, and grew up in Stratford and Oak Hill, Hampstead: "Hopkins had the advantages of the countryside and the largest city in the world. He could go to the galleries, special exhibitions, museums, churches, meetings, open-air spectacles, the London parks, and theatres. As a country boy he became accustomed to trees and open skies."[1] He was also accustomed to winning academic prizes in verse-making, Latin, and history. "I do remember," he recalled at age 34, as a Jesuit priest, "that I was a very conceited boy."[2] By the time he was eighteen, on the cusp of entering Balliol College, Oxford University, he possessed the characteristics for which he would always be known: "the pride, stoicism, eccentricity and vulnerability, the commitment to writing."[3] An outstanding student, fluent in Latin and Greek, he thought he would become a painter, not a common goal for Oxford

---

[1] Norman White. *Hopkins: A Literary Biography.* Oxford: Clarendon Press. 1992. 17.

[2] *The Correspondence of Gerard Manley Hopkins and Richard Watson Dixon.* London: Oxford University Press. 1955. (Letter III. October 5, 1878.) 12.

[3] John McDermott. *A Hopkins Chronology.* New York: St. Martin's Press. 1997. 4.

undergraduates. Fine-featured, sensitive, private, he fought to resist the sensual desires that possessed him. After his first term at Oxford, "Hopkins had given up the idea of becoming a professional artist: he felt that his senses would be dangerously engaged."[4]

As he pursued his studies, he became more and more reflective about and attracted by Roman Catholicism, the attractions that more than twenty years before had led to a high church/low church controversy in the Church of England and John Henry Newman's leaving Oxford for Roman Catholicism. By the time Hopkins was at Oxford, a student going over to Catholicism was rare but not shocking. When Hopkins was twenty, he could envision his own conversion, as disappointing as he knew this would be to his family. Cardinal Newman was the most influential and famous of Victorian England's Catholics, and Hopkins corresponded with him about his desire to join the church. On October 21, 1866, he converted. While Hopkins would not have been admitted to Oxford as a Catholic, he was not forbidden from completing his degree. Newman encouraged the young man but cautioned: "it does not seem to me that there is any hurry about it—your first duty is to make a good class. Show your friends at home that your becoming a Catholic has not unsettled you in the plain duty that lies before you. And, independently of this, it seems to me a better thing not to hurry decision on your vocation. Suffer yourself to be led on by the Grace of God step by step."[5] Hopkins, though, was not one for half-measures, and yearned to join the priesthood. As a test run, Newman invited him to teach at a boys' school in Birmingham in the West Midlands, and the scholarly Hopkins hesitated, unsure if he was cut out for the children's classroom. Teaching and pedagogical administration would be, however, Hopkins's primary religious social service for the rest of his life.

He was almost immediately overwhelmed by the grind of teaching, but, as always, his creative impulses kept flowing, and in the midst of his labors first noted his pet ideas of "inscape" and "instress." During his second term in Birmingham, he reflected in a letter to an Oxford friend: "Teaching is very burdensome, especially when you have so much of it: I have. I have not much time and almost no energy—for I am always tired—to do anything on my own account. ...I want to write still and as a priest I very likely can do that too, not so freely as I shd. have liked, e.g. nothing or little in the verse way, but no

4   Norman White. *Hopkins: A Literary Biography*. Oxford: Clarendon Press. 1992. 147.

5   *Further Letters of Gerard Manley Hopkins.* Edited by Claude Colleer Abbott. 2nd ed. London: Oxford University Press. 1956. (Letter C4. December 6, 1866.) 405.

doubt what wd. best serve the cause of my religion."[6] In the late spring of 1868 he followed through on his resolution to become a priest and chose to become a novice with the Jesuits. Newman told him: "Don't call 'the Jesuit discipline hard,' it will bring you to heaven. The Benedictines would not have suited you."[7] His friends and family tried to respect Gerard's decision, a decision that obviously inconvenienced him more than it could anyone else. Not only would he devote himself to his new religion, but without being asked to do so he would sacrifice his poetry, burning his old drafts (final drafts he preserved or had given to his mother or to his friend Robert Bridges to preserve). He would deny himself the great pleasure of composing verse, unless expressly asked to do so by his superiors. This poetic drought stretched for seven years, with the flow of Hopkins's creative expression running deep underground. Of course, this was the very life he chose; a twentieth-century Jesuit admirer of Hopkins reminds us:

> Let it be plainly stated then at the outset: Religious orders have no crying need of poets; nor, yet again, craving for the honor of their company. Be the poets of major, minor, or mediocre attainments, religious orders flourish grandly like the cedars of Lebanon without them. With them they continue to do so provided the poets in question rest content with their chosen common lot.[8]

Hopkins began his long study and training for the priesthood in 1868 and was assigned to a novitiate in London. After two years, he started his three-year philosophate in Stonyhurst, Lancashire. In 1874, he proceeded in the next stage of his priesthood, moving to St. Beuno's in north Wales, where he may have been happier and more fulfilled than he had ever been before or would be later. He loved the natural environment, the birds, the walks, the *air;* the musicality of the Welsh language, which he set out to learn, became characteristic of his "chiming" verse. It was here, at St. Beuno's, in the midst of his studies, that he was encouraged to write verse again and was able to allow himself brief spells of glorying in poetry. What happened? The New York-bound *SS Deutschland,* carrying more than a hundred passengers, including a group of five nuns exiled from Germany,

---

[6] *Ibid.* (Letter to Alexander Baillie. February 12, 1868.) 231.

[7] *Ibid.* (Letter C13. May 14, 1868.) 407.

[8] Chester A. Burns, S. J. "Gerard Manley Hopkins, Poet of Ascetic and Aesthetic Conflict." In *Immortal Diamond: Studies in Gerard Manley Hopkins.* Edited by Norman Weyand, S. J. New York: Octagon Books. 1969. 176.

foundered in a storm on a sand bar in the mouth of the Thames. The
nuns were among the many who drowned. In Paul Mariani's biography, there is no more thrilling episode than the story of Hopkins's
excited composition of "The Wreck of the Deutschland":

> Perhaps it was on the evening of December 11 [1875] that
> Father Jones saw Hopkins reading the account of the *Deutschland*
> disaster and, seeing how moved he was by what he'd read
> there...did mention in passing—and to comfort the man—that
> it might be nice if someone wrote a poem on the subject,
> especially in light of the witness the tall nun had given in
> her extremity. Whatever hint Jones did drop, it is enough for
> Hopkins, who has been chaffing for years now for just such a
> chance to release himself from his self-imposed exile and begin
> composing again.[9]

And there is no better analysis of Hopkins's weird and wild long
poem than in Elisabeth Schneider's study. She notes:

> The main theme of Part the First is his own conversion; that
> of Part the Second, the hoped-for conversion of all England,
> for which certain events connected with the shipwreck are
> conceived as the spark and the signal. Within the limits of
> its bare thematic frame, however, Hopkins explicitly or by
> implication crowded nearly everything in life about which he
> felt deeply. Reading the poem, one has the feeling that, his
> poetic pen licensed after that decade of largely self-imposed
> silence, he was writing as if he might never again be free to
> write and must set down in this one work all that remained to
> him of value and hope on earth.[10]

After a few months of revision, he submitted "The Wreck of
the Deutschland" to a Catholic magazine, and for several months
expected its publication; finally, the editor, nervous perhaps about
its unconventionality and original theologizing, decided against pre-
senting it to the public. Hopkins thereafter convinced himself that
if his work was meant for publication, it would have to come after
his death.

---

[9] Paul Mariani. *Gerard Manley Hopkins: A Life.* New York: Viking. 2008. 145.

[10] Schneider reminds us that "a lifelong interest in shipwrecks remained one thing
that he could still share with his family. Wrecks...were a main part of the business
of his father, who [was] head of a firm of marine average adjusters..." Elisabeth
W. Schneider. *The Dragon in the Gate: Studies in the Poetry of G. M. Hopkins.*
Berkeley: University of California Press. 1968. 12, 14.

His devoted friend and editor, Robert Bridges, a poet and doctor who collected and recopied almost all of Hopkins's poetic output, endured and countered Hopkins's reproaches, complaints, and criticisms as they explained and argued over each other's poems (including "The Wreck of the Deutschland," which Bridges heartily disliked). When they were not learning from and inspiring each other, they often stamped on each other's literary philosophies and opinions, and, less often, religious differences. The critic Elisabeth Schneider writes: "in spite of extreme temperamental differences Bridges valued Hopkins's work highly though with many qualifications, and... he was a major influence upon the creation of some of the finest of that work. What needs to be noticed...is that the relationship, both personal and literary, was a rewarding but difficult give-and-take affair and that it was Hopkins, not Bridges, who set its critically unsparing tone."[11] Schneider is addressing those who would reproach Bridges for not worshiping and comprehending every word his friend produced. Bridges responded to all of Hopkins's correspondence with intelligence and candor, refusing to agree to understandings he did not have, and usefully asked Hopkins for clarifications. Although Hopkins is not especially articulate or consistent in his explanations of special terms and idiosyncratic forms (for more on "inscape" and "instress," see the footnote below[12]), Bridges's having challenged him on the "oddities" and "obscurities" of the rhythms and phrasings helped Hopkins illuminate for himself and thus in his poetry his primary purposes:

> Why do I employ sprung rhythm at all? Because it is the nearest to the speech of prose, that is the native and natural rhythm of speech, the least forced, the most rhetorical and emphatic of all possible rhythms, combining, as it seems

---

[11] Elisabeth W. Schneider. *The Dragon in the Gate: Studies in the Poetry of G. M. Hopkins.* Berkeley: University of California Press. 1968. 130.

[12] Professor Schneider does her best to weigh and clarify Hopkins's special terms: "*Inscape*...may be roughly described as organic form with emphasis on the individuality implicit in the organic. Though the term itself does not occur in Hopkins's poetry, his preoccupation with what it represents is an underlying principle in all his work; the particular word scarcely matters, but that he felt so strongly about the concept that he had to invent his own name for it is significant. The term *instress* presents a more difficult problem. It occurs twice in the poems...and many times elsewhere, appearing as both verb and substantive, in religious contexts and with reference to natural beauty. Sometimes it seems to be a property of the object; at other times it appears as the effect of the object on the human or supernatural being...Always the term has something to do with emphasis, but beyond that I can be sure of no single, consistently maintained meaning." Elisabeth W. Schneider. *The Dragon in the Gate: Studies in the Poetry of G. M. Hopkins.* Berkeley: University of California Press. 1968. 118.

to me, opposite and, one wd. have thought, incompatible
excellences, markedness of rhythm—that is rhythm's self—and
naturalness of expression—for why, if it is forcible in prose
to say "lashed: rod," am I obliged to weaken this in verse,
which ought to be stronger, not weaker, into "láshed birch-
ród" or something?[13]

In this same letter, following that impatient outburst, he scolds
Bridges, as he may well have scolded us on our first baffled encoun-
ters with his strange and glorious verse:

> My verse is less to be read than heard, as I have told you
> before; it is oratorical, that is the rhythm is so. I think if you
> will study what I have here said you will be much more pleased
> with it and may I say? converted to it....
> I cannot think of altering anything. Why shd. I? I do not write
> for the public. You are my public and I hope to convert you.
> You say you wd. not for any money read my poem again.
> Nevertheless I beg you will. Besides money, you know, there
> is love. If it is obscure do not bother yourself with the meaning
> but pay attention to the best and most intelligible stanzas, as
> the two last of each part and the narrative of the wreck. If you
> had done this you wd. have liked it better and sent me some
> serviceable criticisms, but now your criticism is of no use, being
> only a protest memorializing me against my whole policy and
> proceedings.[14]

The advice in the last paragraph ("If it is obscure do not bother
yourself with the meaning but pay attention to the best and most
intelligible stanzas,") though unheeded by a stubborn Bridges, is for
the rest of us well-worth taking.

Free to write again, and with Wales inspiring him, he composed
some of his most beautiful and rhythmically inventive poems, among
them "God's Grandeur," "The Windhover," "Pied Beauty," and "The
Lantern out of Doors." His walks and observations created impres-
sions that he would set down and then voice into shape:

> Summer ends now; now, barbarous in beauty, the stooks arise
>   Around; up above, what wind-walks! what lovely behaviour
>   Of silk-sack clouds! Has wilder, willful-wavier
> Meal-drift moulded ever and melted across skies?
>
>   ("Hurrahing in Harvest")

---

[13] *The Letters of Gerard Manley Hopkins to Robert Bridges*. London: Oxford University
   Press. 1935. (Letter XXXVII, August 21, 1877.) 46.
[14] *Ibid.*

He seems to have composed while hearing internal melodies and rhythms. He explained to the poet and canon Richard Watson Dixon one of his discoveries that preceded the composition of "The Wreck of the Deutschland": "I had long had haunting my ear the echo of a new rhythm which now I realised on paper. To speak shortly, it consists in scanning by accents or stresses alone, without any account of syllables, so that a foot may be one strong syllable or it may be many light and one strong. I do not say the idea is altogether new; there are hints of it in music, in nursery rhymes and popular jingles…"[15] When he added stress marks in particular poems and lines he meant to clarify their reading, but they did and do often confuse: "Even with the aid of Hopkins's indications of stress," writes Professor Schneider, "it is difficult to determine how some of the lines—'So tiny a trickle of sóng-strain' is an example—were meant to be stressed or timed; and, intention apart, no satisfactory, undistorted reading seems possible."[16]

And while his writing often seems ahead of its time, so that some find it "modernist," he did not write obscurely on purpose; he meant to present his hard-won realizations clearly. He would say, however, that clarity sometimes comes only with some hard looking. During a sermon in 1880 (Mariani narrates), Hopkins "exhorts his brethren to pay close attention to the words he has to say, and not 'to stare or sleep over them but to heed them,' for it is both 'contemptible and unmanly…for men whose minds are naturally clear, to give up at the first hearing of a hard passage in the Scripture…to care to know no more than children know.'"[17]

Less important to Hopkins than explicating his metrical ideas was promoting an active and aural experience of his poems:

> …remember what applies to all my verse, that it is, as living art should be, made for performance and that its performance is not reading with the eye but loud, leisurely, poetical (not rhetorical) recitation, with long rests, long dwells on the rhyme and other marked syllables…[18]

[15] *The Correspondence of Gerard Manley Hopkins and Richard Watson Dixon.* London: Oxford University Press. 1955. (Letter III. October 5–10, 1878.) 14.

[16] Elisabeth W. Schneider. *The Dragon in the Gate: Studies in the Poetry of G. M. Hopkins.* Berkeley: University of California Press. 1968. 84.

[17] Paul Mariani. *Gerard Manley Hopkins: A Life.* New York: Viking. 2008. 245.

[18] *The Letters of Gerard Manley Hopkins to Robert Bridges.* London: Oxford University Press. 1935. (Letter CXLIII, December 11, 1886.) 246.

The rhythm of "Harry Ploughman" he told Bridges: "is altogether for recital, and not for perusal (as by nature verse should be)."[19] So, his poems can *look* difficult but their sound is a natural clarifier; even so, there are many lines and phrases that have resisted satisfactory analysis. There are also, it should be said, completely finished and transparent poems of *little* weight and, then again, there are fragments as evocative as those torn stanzas of the ancient Greek poets.[20] There are surprises everywhere.

Anxious as he was about the lusts and desires of his own body, Hopkins marveled at and delighted in the soaring and gliding and flickering of God's winged creatures:

> I caught this morning morning's minion, king-
>> dom of daylight's dauphin, dapple-dawn-drawn Falcon, in his riding
>> Of the rolling level underneath him steady air, and striding
> High there, how he run upon the rein of a wimpling wing
> In his ecstasy! then off, off forth on swing,
>> As a skate's heel sweeps smooth on a bow-bend: the hurl and gliding
>> Rebuffed the big wind. My heart in hiding
> Stirred for a bird,—the achieve of, the mastery of the thing!

> ("The Windhover")

The intense and broody and slow-churning Hopkins is *the* ecstatic poet of the nineteenth century, outstepping even his prolific cross-Atlantic secular rival, Walt Whitman, whose thrilled appreciations of Democracy's men and women and self seem comparatively pre-meditated. Hopkins's two primary readers in his lifetime reacted to their friend's ecstasy by being "carried away" by it themselves. Dixon wrote Hopkins:

> ...I cannot but take courage to hope that the day will come,
> when so health-breathing and purely powerful a faculty as you
> have been gifted with may find its proper issue in the world.
> Bridges struck the truth long ago when he said to me that your

---

[19] Bridges quotes from this letter in his note to No. 43, "Harry Ploughman." See as well *The Letters of Gerard Manley Hopkins to Robert Bridges*. London: Oxford University Press. 1935. (Letter CLIII, October 11, 1887.) 263.

[20] There does not seem to be, however, an easy or obvious distinction between his "nature" poems and "religious" poems. Nature continuously illuminated his religious understanding and appreciation and vice versa. There may be a distinction, however, between those poems arising from personal observation and experience and those contrived from literary or imaginative sources. His attempts at dramatization and characterization (see, for example, "The Bugler's First Communion") are always earnest but only sometimes convincing.

poems more carried him out of himself than those of any one. I
have again and again felt the same: & am certain that as a means
of serving, I will not say your cause, but religion, you cannot
have a more powerful instrument than your own verses.[21]

Such alluring praise Hopkins fought off, and to the end of his life
he continued to suppress his calling as a poet for his chosen work
as a priest.[22] The trickle of poems in the last eighteen years of his
life were blood sacrifices, were stolen, he sometimes felt, from his
duty and submission to God. Verse-making was a Siren's call. He
explains to Dixon:

> I am ashamed at the expressions of high regard which your
> last letter and others have contained, kind and touching as they
> are, and do not know whether I ought to reply to them or not.
> This I say: my vocation puts before me a standard so high that
> a higher can be found nowhere else. The question then for
> me is not whether I am willing (if I may guess what is in your
> mind) to make a sacrifice of hopes of fame (let us suppose),
> but whether I am not to undergo a severe judgment from God
> for the lothness I have shewn in making it, for the reserves I
> may have in my heart made, for the backward glances I have
> given with my hand upon the plough, for the waste of time
> the very compositions you admire may have caused and their
> preoccupation of the mind which belonged to more sacred
> or more binding duties, for the disquiet and the thoughts of
> vainglory they may have given rise to.[23]

---

[21] *The Correspondence of Gerard Manley Hopkins and Richard Watson Dixon.* London: Oxford University Press. 1955. (Letter XXII A: January 28, 1882.) 100.

[22] "Suppress," anyway, is how his friends and many literary admirers see it. From the perspective of the Society of Jesus, says Chester A. Burns, it looks different: "A Jesuit poet in last analysis is no more than any given Jesuit, supposing such talent, giving God glory through the exercise of his poetic gifts. When there is a question of poetry setting up court for itself, and danger thereby of God's glory being impinged on, danger in fact of that glory being not at all sought, the Jesuit poet must draw swiftly back; else he is in so far no true Jesuit, no authentic follower of Him Whom he has proposed to himself as his leader supreme in life: Christ the Lord." (Chester A. Burns, S. J. "Gerard Manley Hopkins, Poet of Ascetic and Aesthetic Conflict." In *Immortal Diamond: Studies in Gerard Manley Hopkins.* Edited by Norman Weyand, S. J. New York: Octagon Books. 1969. 183.)

[23] *The Correspondence of Gerard Manley Hopkins and Richard Watson Dixon.* London: Oxford University Press. 1955. (Letter XXI: October 28–November 2, 1881.) 88.

Back to work he went, but the relentless forces he applied or sought to have applied to himself were terrible, and there were times where he knew he was overdoing it, grinding himself down, in penitence, in service:

> My own heart let me have more pity on; let
> Me live to my sad self hereafter kind,
> Charitable; not live this tormented mind
> With this tormented mind tormenting yet.

> ("My own heart")

The biographer Paul Mariani observes: "…there is something in Hopkins that keeps fighting his own extraordinary creativity, keeping it under an adamantine compression so intense that it has even affected his physical well-being. Sacrifice is all, he keeps telling himself. Making of oneself an acceptable sacrifice. But in his self-immolation, he has provided a space for an intense flame, which will burn away the dross to leave behind a scattering of diamonds to be lifted by others from the ashes of time."[24] Hopkins reflects on that "diamond" theme in "That Nature is a Heraclitean Fire and of the comfort of the Resurrection":

> …Flesh fade, and mortal trash
> Fall to the residuary worm; | world's wildfire, leave but ash:
>   In a flash, at a trumpet crash,
> I am all at once what Christ is, | since he was what I am, and
> This Jack, joke, poor potsherd,| patch, matchwood, immortal diamond,
>   Is immortal diamond.

Finally, or usually, in reading of his life or experiencing his darker poems, we are left awed or aghast; we are the horrified but sympathetic citizens of Thebes who witness Oedipus' sufferings, his wanderings after his self-inflicted blindness. Hopkins's self-judgments are servere:

> I am gall, I am heartburn. God's most deep decree
> Bitter would have me taste: my taste was me;
> Bones built in me, flesh filled, blood brimmed the curse.

> ("I wake and feel the fell of dark, not day")

---

[24] Paul Mariani. *Gerard Manley Hopkins: A Life.* New York: Viking. 2008. 280.

Hopkins would go his own way as a man and artist, even if, at various times, his torments seemed to him a folly, an attempted grandeur in a world of small details. But, O, how he loved the vital details of divine powers!

> The world is charged with the grandeur of God.
>   It will flame out, like shining from shook foil;
>   It gathers to a greatness, like the ooze of oil
> Crushed....

So, thanks to Bridges's careful preservation and presentation of his friend's poems, we readers of the twenty-first century get to experience, more than perhaps from any other religiously devoted poet, not only the ecstasy and agony of religious discipline but the joyful appreciations of "God's Grandeur":

> And for all this, nature is never spent;
>   There lives the dearest freshness deep down things;
> And though the last lights off the black West went
>   Oh, morning, at the brown brink eastward, springs—

> ("God's Grandeur")

Nature, which Hopkins would never have distinguished from God's creation, could bring him out of himself, could "blossom" him out of his cranky, absorbed, tortured self:

> Lovely the woods, waters, meadows, combes, vales,
> All the air things wear that build this world of Wales...

> ("In the Valley of the Elwy")

In 1877, at the end of his training in Wales, he failed to pass highly enough on his exams to continue his studies; he was ordained a priest but not of the highest rank: "And though he is heartsick over the news, he will keep this to himself like the good soldier he is and serve wherever he is sent."[25] What he didn't count on was the relentless mental application and poor health that he would face as a spiritual worker in England and Ireland's immigrant and Catholic communities.

He was sent and positioned here and there, as needed, from St. Mary's College in Chesterfield to Stonyhurst, to London, to the Oxford slums, and from there to Lancashire and soon after to Liverpool, and then back again to Stonyhurst to coach students for their classics exams. "I like my pupils," he wrote his Oxford University friend Alexander Baillie, "and do not wholly dislike the

---

[25] Paul Mariani. *Gerard Manley Hopkins: A Life.* New York: Viking. 2008. 182.

work, but I fall into or continue in a heavy weary state of body and mind in which my go is gone...I make no way with what I read, and seem but half a man."[26] He felt other priests could have made something more with their limited free time, but practicality and efficiency had never been his way: "My time, as I have said before this, is not so closely employed but that someone else in my place might not do a good deal, but I cannot, and I see no grounded prospect of my ever doing much not only in poetry but in anything at all."[27] In fits and starts, he continued to compose startling verses from his passionately searching point of view. He strove for peace, for spiritual comfort, but usually had to remind himself that even when it came, contented reflection was not to be his lot in this world:

> ...And when Peace here does house
> He comes with work to do, he does not come to coo,
> He comes to brood and sit.

("Peace")

His family and friends only rarely heard tell of the rigors he underwent and his low spirits. Apologizing for a long lapse in correspondence, he tells Bridges:

> But I never could write; time and spirits were wanting; one is so fagged, so harried and gallied up and down. And the drunkards go on drinking, the filthy, as the scripture says, are filthy still: human nature is so inveterate. Would that I had seen the last of it.[28]

In February of 1884 he was sent to University College, Dublin, as Fellow in Classics and Professor of Greek and Latin literature, but it was anything but a plum job. His teaching and marking were overwhelming, and his housing was squalid. For the next five years he would work more doggedly and feel more depressed than ever. "The melancholy I have all my life been subject to," he writes Baillie, "has become of late years not indeed more intense in its fits but rather more distributed, constant, and crippling. One, the lightest but a very inconvenient form of it, is daily anxiety about work to be

---

[26] *Further Letters of Gerard Manley Hopkins.* Edited by Claude Colleer Abbott. 2nd ed. London: Oxford University Press. 1956. (Letter of January 14, 1883.) 251.

[27] *The Correspondence of Gerard Manley Hopkins and Richard Watson Dixon.* London: Oxford University Press. 1955. (Letter XXVII. June 25, 1883.) 108.

[28] *The Letters of Gerard Manley Hopkins to Robert Bridges.* London: Oxford University Press. 1935. (Letter LXX, October 26, 1880.) 110.

done, which makes me break off or never finish all that lies outside that work....I see no ground for thinking I shall ever get over it or ever succeed in doing anything that is not forced on me to do of any consequence."[29]

> The times are nightfall, look, their light grows less;
> The times are winter, watch, a world undone:
> They waste, they wither worse; they as they run
> Or bring more or more blazon man's distress.
> And I not help. Nor word now of success:
> All is from wreck, here, there, to rescue one—
> Work which to see scarce so much as begun
> Makes welcome death, does dear forgetfulness.

("The times are nightfall")

When he died of typhoid on June 8, 1889, he was forty-four and as a poet completely unknown to the world. Several decades after his death he became one of the most famous and appreciated of Victorian-era poets.[30]

It was not until 1918, after Bridges had placed a number of Hopkins's poems in anthologies, that Bridges published *Poems of Gerard Manley Hopkins*. Other poems and other versions of the poems therein have come to light since.[31] This edition contains all of the poems and fragments as arranged by Bridges, as well as Bridges's preface and lengthy notes. Also presented here is Hopkins's own preface, which Bridges believes he wrote in 1883; while interesting, more illuminating are the excerpts from Hopkins's letters that Bridges quotes in the notes. Bridges's notes, by the way, were discretely placed as endnotes in the original edition. I have placed them as footnotes for their readier use.[32]

---

[29] *Further Letters of Gerard Manley Hopkins*. Edited by Claude Colleer Abbott. 2nd ed. London: Oxford University Press. 1956. (May 8, 1885 in the letter dated April 24.) 256.

[30] Hopkins's verse has been studied at almost molecular level, and he may well now be the most thoroughly analyzed (mentally, biographically, versibly) English poet of his time, surpassing even his long-lived contemporary Thomas Hardy (1840–1928). He is certainly much more highly regarded than his friend Robert Bridges. It should be said that if the flash and power of the famous poems do not strike a reader's senses, learning about the poetry's rhythmical and theological subtleties is not likely going to bring about an illuminating current of understanding.

[31] See, for one, Catherine Phillips's *Gerard Manley Hopkins: The Major Works*.

[32] If some of the notes are arcane, they allow us to see the difficulties Bridges faced as a transcriber and compiler of various versions of the poems; many of the notes are delightfully candid commentaries; best of all are the relevant excerpts from Hopkins's letters to Bridges and R. W. Dixon.

What a reader should do, however, before turning to myriad sources for explications of the poems is this (as Hopkins advised the confused readers in his lifetime): Take some pains and prepare as a musician would prepare, so to understand the movements. Then, try again, and "take breath and read it with the ears, as I always wish to be read, and my verse becomes all right."[33]

*

Bibliographical Note

My primary sources are given in this introduction's footnotes. My education in Hopkins's life relies most heavily on Paul Mariani's extraordinarily compelling biography, which I enthusiastically recommend. Norman White's biography, on the other hand, while much more thoroughly covering Hopkins's childhood, boyhood, and youth, suffers from an irritated disillusionment with its subject. John McDermott's *A Hopkins Chronology* is, like others in Macmillan's Author Chronologies series, wonderful. Elisabeth Schneider's study of Hopkins is boldly commonsensical and unusually tactful and modest. I have learned from her book what, had I been born a dozen years earlier, I may have been able to learn from her in a graduate seminar at University of California, Santa Barbara. Joaquin Kuhn and Joseph J. Feeney's *Hopkins Variations: Standing Round a Waterfall* (Philadelphia and New York: St. Joseph's University Press and Fordham University Press, 2002) is a collection of fine short essays about various Hopkins devotees' introductions to the poetry. Finally I would like to thank Frances Stephens, widow of the poet Alan Stephens (1925–2009), whom I loved and with whom I studied for many years, for lending me his exquisitely noted and referenced copy of John Pick's *A Hopkins Reader* (Garden City, New York: Image Books, 1966).

★ ★ ★

—*Bob Blaisdell*

---

[33] *The Letters of Gerard Manley Hopkins to Robert Bridges*. London: Oxford University Press. 1935. (Letter LIX, April 22, 1879.) 79.

Dedicatory Poem

Our generation already is overpast,
And thy lov'd legacy, Gerard, hath lain
Coy in my home; as once thy heart was fain
Of shelter, when God's terror held thee fast
In life's wild wood at Beauty and Sorrow aghast;
Thy sainted sense tramme'd in ghostly pain,
Thy rare ill-broker'd talent in disdain:
Yet love of Christ will win man's love at last.

Hell wars without; but, dear, the while my hands
Gather'd thy book, I heard, this wintry day,
Thy spirit thank me, in his young delight
Stepping again upon the yellow sands.
Go forth: amidst our chaffinch flock display
Thy plumage of far wonder and heavenward flight!

—Robert Bridges
Chilswell, Jan. 1918.

~

Preface[34]

by Gerard Manley Hopkins (c. 1883)

~

The poems in this book[35] are written some in Running Rhythm, the common rhythm in English use, some in Sprung Rhythm, and some in a mixture of the two. And those in the common rhythm are some counterpointed, some not.

Common English rhythm, called Running Rhythm above, is measured by feet of either two or three syllables and (putting aside the imperfect feet at the beginning and end of lines and also some unusual measures, in which feet seem to be paired together and double or composite feet to arise) never more or less.

Every foot has one principal stress or accent, and this or the syllable it falls on may be called the Stress of the foot and the other part, the one or two unaccented syllables, the Slack. Feet (and the rhythms made out of them) in which the stress comes first are called Falling Feet and Falling Rhythms, feet and rhythm in which the slack comes first are called Rising Feet and Rhythms, and if the stress is between two slacks there will be Rocking Feet and Rhythms. These distinctions are real and true to nature; but for purposes of scanning it is a great convenience to follow the example of music and take the stress always first, as the accent or the chief accent always comes first in a musical bar. If this is done there will be in common English verse

---

[34] This is from B [see Bridges's Preface to Notes, page xxvii], and must have been written in '83 or not much later. [Note by R. Bridges.]

[35] That is, the manuscript described in [Bridges's Preface to Notes, [page xxvii] as B. *This* preface does not apply to the early poems. [Note by R. Bridges.]

only two possible feet—the so-called accentual Trochee and Dactyl, and correspondingly only two possible uniform rhythms, the so-called Trochaic and Dactylic. But they may be mixed and then what the Greeks called a Logaoedic Rhythm arises. These are the facts and according to these the scanning of ordinary regularly-written English verse is very simple indeed and to bring in other principles is here unnecessary.

But because verse written strictly in these feet and by these principles will become same and tame the poets have brought in licences and departures from rule to give variety, and especially when the natural rhythm is rising, as in the common ten-syllable or five-foot verse, rhymed or blank. These irregularities are chiefly Reversed Feet and Reversed or Counterpoint Rhythm, which two things are two steps or degrees of licence in the same kind. By a reversed foot I mean the putting the stress where, to judge by the rest of the measure, the slack should be and the slack where the stress, and this is done freely at the beginning of a line and, in the course of a line, after a pause; only scarcely ever in the second foot or place and never in the last, unless when the poet designs some extraordinary effect; for these places are characteristic and sensitive and cannot well be touched. But the reversal of the first foot and of some middle foot after a strong pause is a thing so natural that our poets have generally done it, from Chaucer down, without remark and it commonly passes unnoticed and cannot be said to amount to a formal change of rhythm, but rather is that irregularity which all natural growth and motion shews. If however the reversal is repeated in two feet running, especially so as to include the sensitive second foot, it must be due either to great want of ear or else is a calculated effect, the superinducing or mounting of a new rhythm upon the old; and since the new or mounted rhythm is actually heard and at the same time the mind naturally supplies the natural or standard foregoing rhythm, for we do not forget what the rhythm is that by rights we should be hearing, two rhythms are in some manner running at once and we have something answerable to counterpoint in music, which is two or more strains of tune going on together, and this is Counterpoint Rhythm. Of this kind of verse Milton is the great master and the choruses of *Samson Agonistes* are written throughout in it—but with the disadvantage that he does not let the reader clearly know what the ground-rhythm is meant to be and so they have struck most readers as merely irregular. And in fact if you counterpoint throughout, since one only of the counter rhythms is actually heard, the other is really destroyed or cannot come to exist, and what is written is one rhythm only and probably Sprung Rhythm, of which I now speak.

Sprung Rhythm, as used in this book, is measured by feet of from one to four syllables, regularly, and for particular effects any number of weak or slack syllables may be used. It has one stress, which falls on the only syllable, if there is only one, or, if there are more, then scanning as above, on the first, and so gives rise to four sorts of feet, a monosyllable and the so-called accentual Trochee, Dactyl, and the First Paeon. And there will be four corresponding natural rhythms; but nominally the feet are mixed and any one may follow any other. And hence Sprung Rhythm differs from Running Rhythm in having or being only one nominal rhythm, a mixed or "logaoedic" one, instead of three, but on the other hand in having twice the flexibility of foot, so that any two stresses may either follow one another running or be divided by one, two, or three slack syllables. But strict Sprung Rhythm cannot be counterpointed. In Sprung Rhythm, as in logaoedic rhythm generally, the feet are assumed to be equally long or strong and their seeming inequality is made up by pause or stressing.

Remark also that it is natural in Sprung Rhythm for the lines to be *rove over*,[36] that is for the scanning of each line immediately to take up that of the one before, so that if the first has one or more syllables at its end the other must have so many the less at its beginning; and in fact the scanning runs on without break from the beginning, say, of a stanza to the end and all the stanza is one long strain, though written in lines asunder.

Two licences are natural to Sprung Rhythm. The one is rests, as in music; but of this an example is scarcely to be found in this book, unless in the *Echos,* second line. The other is *hangers* or *outrides* that is one, two, or three slack syllables added to a foot and not counting in the nominal scanning. They are so called because they seem to hang below the line or ride forward or backward from it in another dimension than the line itself, according to a principle needless to explain here. These outriding half feet or hangers are marked by a loop underneath them, and plenty of them will be found.[37]

The other marks are easily understood, namely accents, where the reader might be in doubt which syllable should have the stress; slurs, that is loops *over* syllables, to tie them together into the time of one; little loops at the end of a line to shew that the rhyme goes on to the

---

[36] This expression is used here to denote the running on of the sense and sound of the end of a verse into the beginning of the next; but this meaning is not easily to be found in the word. [Note by R. Bridges.]

[37] Bridges did not use Hopkins's guiding "loops" in his edition.

first letter of the next line; what in music are called pauses, to shew that the syllable should be dwelt on; and twirls, to mark reversed or counterpointed rhythm.[38]

Note on the nature and history of Sprung Rhythm—Sprung Rhythm is the most natural of things. For (1) it is the rhythm of common speech and of written prose, when rhythm is perceived in them. (2) It is the rhythm of all but the most monotonously regular music, so that in the words of choruses and refrains and in songs written closely to music it arises. (3) It is found in nursery rhymes, weather saws, and so on; because, however these may have been once made in running rhythm, the terminations having dropped off by the change of language, the stresses come together and so the rhythm is sprung. (4) It arises in common verse when reversed or counterpointed, for the same reason.

But nevertheless in spite of all this and though Greek and Latin lyric verse, which is well known, and the old English verse seen in *Pierce Ploughman* are in sprung rhythm, it has in fact ceased to be used since the Elizabethan age, [Robert] Greene being the last writer who can be said to have recognised it. For perhaps there was not, down to our days, a single, even short, poem in English in which sprung rhythm is employed not for single effects or in fixed places but as the governing principle of the scansion. I say this because the contrary has been asserted: if it is otherwise the poem should be cited.

*

Some of the sonnets in this book are in five-foot, some in six-foot or Alexandrine lines.

Nos. 13 and 22 are Curtal-Sonnets, that is they are constructed in proportions resembling those of the sonnet proper, namely 6 + 4 instead of 8 + 6, with however a halfline tailpiece (so that the equation is rather $12/8+9/2=21/2+10\ 1/2$).

*

---

[38] Bridges represented some of Hopkins's accent marks but none of the "slurs," "little loops," or "twirls."

Preface to NOTES

by Robert Bridges (1918)

≈

An editor of posthumous work is bounden to give some account of the authority for his text; and it is the purpose of the following notes to satisfy inquiry concerning matters whereof the present editor has the advantage of first-hand or particular knowledge. The sources are four, and will he distinguished as A, B, D, and H, as here described.

A is my own collection, a MS. book made up of autographs—by which word I denote poems in the author's handwriting—pasted into it as they were received from him, and also of contemporary copies of other poems. These autographs and copies date from '67 to '89, the year of his death. Additions made by copying after that date are not reckoned or used. The two facsimiles are cuttings from A.

B is a MS. book, into which, in '83, I copied from A certain poems of which the author had kept no copy. He was remiss in making fair copies of his work, and his autograph of "The Deutschland" having been (seemingly) lost, I copied that poem and others from A at his request. After that date he entered more poems in this book as he completed them, and he also made both corrections of copy and emendations of the poems which had been copied into it by me. Thus, if a poem occur in both A and B, then B is the later and, except for overlooked errors of copyist, the better authority. The last entry written by G. M. H. into this book is of the date 1887.

D is a collection of the author's letters to Canon [Richard Watson] Dixon, the only other friend who ever read his poems, with but few exceptions whether of persons or of poems. These letters are in my keeping; they contain autographs of a few poems with late corrections.

H is the bundle of posthumous papers that came into my hands at the author's death. These were at the time examined, sorted, and indexed; and the more important pieces—of which copies were taken—were inserted into a scrap-book. That collection is the source of a series of his most mature sonnets, and of almost all the unfinished poems and fragments. Among these papers were also some early drafts. The facsimiles *a* and *b* are from H [see poem No. 67, "On a piece of music," page 81].

The latest autographs and autographic corrections have been preferred. In the very few instances in which this principle was overruled, as in Nos.1 and 27, the justification will be found in the note to the poem. The finished poems from 1 to 51 are ranged chronologically by the years, but in the section 52-74 a fanciful grouping of the fragments was preferred to the inevitable misrepresentations of conjectural dating. G. M. H. dated his poems from their inception, and however much he revised a poem he would date his recast as his first draft. Thus "Handsome Heart" was written and sent to me in '79; and the recast, which I reject, was not made before '83, while the final corrections may be some years later; and yet his last autograph is dated as the first "Oxford '79."

This edition purports to convey all the author's serious mature poems; and he would probably not have wished any of his earlier poems nor so many of his fragments to have been included. Of the former class three specimens only are admitted—and these, which may be considered of exceptional merit or interest, had already been given to the public—but of the latter almost everything; because these scraps being of mature date, generally contain some special beauty of thought or diction, and are invariably of metrical or rhythmical interest: some of them are in this respect as remarkable as anything in the volume. As for exclusion, no translations of any kind are published here, whether into Greek or Latin from the English—of which there are autographs and copies in A—or the Englishing of Latin hymns—occurring in H—: these last are not in my opinion of special merit; and with them I class a few religious pieces which will be noticed later.

Of the peculiar scheme of prosody invented and developed by the author a full account is out of the question. His own preface together with his description of the metrical scheme of each poem—which is always, wherever it exists, transcribed in the notes—may be a sufficient guide for practical purposes. Moreover, the intention of the rhythm, in places where it might seem doubtful, has been indicated by accents printed over the determining syllables: in the later poems these accents correspond generally with the author's own marks; in the earlier poems they do not, but are trustworthy translations.

It was at one time the author's practice to use a very elaborate system of marks, all indicating the speech-movement: the autograph (in A) of "Harry Ploughman" carries seven different marks, each one defined at the foot. When reading through his letters for the purpose of determining dates, I noted a few sentences on this subject which will justify the method that I have followed in the text. In 1883 he wrote: "You were right to leave out the marks: they were not consistent for one thing, and are always offensive. Still there must be some. Either I must invent a notation applied throughout as in music or else I must only mark where the reader is likely to mistake, and for the present this is what I shall do." And again in '85: "This is my difficulty, what marks to use and when to use them: they are so much needed and yet so objectionable. About punctuation my mind is clear: I can give a rule for everything I write myself, and even for other people, though they might not agree with me perhaps." In this last matter the autographs are rigidly respected, the rare intentional aberration being scrupulously noted. And so I have respected his indentation of the verse; but in the sonnets, while my indentation corresponds, as a rule, with some autograph, I have felt free to consider conveniences, following, however, his growing practice to eschew it altogether.

Apart from questions of taste—and if these poems were to be arraigned for errors of what may be called taste, they might be convicted of occasional affectation in metaphor, as where the hills are "as a stallion stalwart, very-violet-sweet," or of some perversion of human feeling, as, for instance, the "nostrils' relish of incense along the sanctuary side," or "the Holy Ghost with warm breast and with ah! bright wings," these and a few such examples are mostly efforts to force emotion into theological or sectarian channels, as in "the comfortless unconfessed" and the unpoetic line "His mystery must be unstressed stressed," or, again, the exaggerated Marianism of some pieces, or the naked encounter of sensualism and asceticism which hurts the "Golden Echo."—

Apart, I say, from such faults of taste, which few as they numerically are yet affect my liking and more repel my sympathy than do all the rude shocks of his purely artistic wantonness—apart from these there are definite faults of style which a reader must have courage to face, and must in some measure condone before he can discover the great beauties. For these blemishes in the poet's style are of such quality and magnitude as to deny him even a hearing from those who love a continuous literary decorum and are grown to be intolerant of its absence. And it is well to be clear that there is no pretence to reverse the condemnation of those faults, for which the poet has duly suffered. The extravagances are and will remain what they were. Nor can credit be gained from pointing them out: yet, to put readers at their ease, I will here define them: they may be called Oddity and Obscurity; and since the first may provoke laughter when a writer is serious (and this poet is always serious), while the latter must prevent him from being understood (and this poet has always something to say), it may be assumed that they were not a part of his intention.

Something of what he thought on this subject may be seen in the following extracts from his letters. In Feb. 1879, he wrote: "All therefore that I think of doing is to keep my verses together in one place—at present I have not even correct copies—, that, if anyone should like, they might be published after my death. And that again is unlikely, as well as remote.... No doubt my poetry errs on the side of oddness. I hope in time to have a more balanced and Miltonic style. But as air, melody, is what strikes me most of all in music and design in painting, so design, pattern, or what I am in the habit of calling *inscape* is what I above all aim at in poetry. Now it is the virtue of design, pattern, or inscape to be distinctive and it is the vice of distinctiveness to become queer. This vice I cannot have escaped." And again two months later: "Moreover the oddness may make them repulsive at first and yet Lang might have liked them on a second reading. Indeed when, on somebody returning me the *Eurydice,* I opened and read some lines, as one commonly reads whether prose or verse, with the eyes, so to say, only, it struck me aghast with a kind of raw nakedness and unmitigated violence I was unprepared for: but take breath and read it with the ears, as I always wish to be read, and my verse becomes all right."

As regards Oddity then, it is plain that the poet was himself fully alive to it, but he was not sufficiently aware of his obscurity, and he could not understand why his friends found his sentences so difficult: he would never have believed that, among all the ellipses and liberties of his grammar, the one chief cause is his habitual omission of the relative pronoun; and yet this is so, and the examination of a simple example or two may serve a general purpose:

This grammatical liberty, though it is a common convenience in conversation and has therefore its proper place in good writing, is apt to confuse the parts of speech, and to reduce a normal sequence of words to mere jargon. Writers who carelessly rely on their elliptical speech-forms to govern the elaborate sentences of their literary composition little know what a conscious effort of interpretation they often impose on their readers. But it was not carelessness in Gerard Hopkins: he had full skill and practice and scholarship in conventional forms, and it is easy to see that he banished these purely constructional syllables from his verse because they took up room which he thought he could not afford them: he needed in his scheme all his space for his poetical words, and he wished those to crowd out every merely grammatical colourless or toneless element; and so when he had got into the habit of doing without these relative pronouns—though he must, I suppose, have supplied them in his thought,—he abuses the licence beyond precedent, as when he writes (no. 17) "O Hero savest!" for "O Hero that savest!"

Another example of this (from the 5th stanza of no. 23) will discover another cause of obscurity; the line

> Squander the hell-rook ranks sally to molest him

means "Scatter the ranks that sally to molest him": but since the words *squander* and *sally* occupy similar positions in the two sections of the verse, and are enforced by a similar accentuation, the second verb deprived of its pronoun will follow the first and appear as an imperative; and there is nothing to prevent its being so taken but the contradiction that it makes in the meaning; whereas the grammar should expose and enforce the meaning, not have to be determined by the meaning. Moreover, there is no way of enunciating this line which will avoid the confusion; because if, knowing that *sally* should not have the same intonation as *squander,* the reader mitigates the accent, and in doing so lessens or obliterates the caesural pause which exposes its accent, then *ranks* becomes a genitive and *sally* a substantive.

Here, then, is another source of the poet's obscurity; that in aiming at condensation he neglects the need that there is for care in the placing of words that are grammatically ambiguous. English swarms with words that have one identical form for substantive, adjective, and verb; and such a word should never be so placed as to allow of any doubt as to what part of speech it is used for; because such ambiguity or momentary uncertainty destroys the force of the sentence. Now our author not only neglects this essential propriety but he would seem even to welcome and seek artistic effect in the consequent confusion; and he will sometimes so arrange such words that a reader looking for a verb may find that he has two or three ambiguous monosyllables from which to select, and must be in doubt as to which promises best to give any meaning that he can welcome; and then, after his choice is made, he may be left with some homeless monosyllable still on his hands. Nor is our author apparently sensitive to the irrelevant suggestions that our numerous homophones cause; and he will provoke further ambiguities or obscurities by straining the meaning of these unfortunate words.

Finally, the rhymes where they are peculiar are often repellent, and so far from adding charm to the verse that they appear as obstacles. This must not blind one from recognizing that Gerard Hopkins, where he is simple and straightforward in his rhyme is a master of it—there are many instances,—but when he indulges in freaks, his childishness is incredible. His intention in such places is that the verses should be recited running on without pause, and the rhyme occurring in their midst should be like a phonetic accident, merely satisfying the prescribed form. But his phonetic rhymes are often indefensible on his own principle. The rhyme to *communion* in "The Bugler" is hideous, and the suspicion that the poet thought it ingenious is appalling; *eternal,* in "The Eurydice," does not correspond with *burn all,* and in "Felix Randal" *and some* and *handsome* is as truly an eye-rhyme as the *love* and *prove* which he despised and abjured;—and it is more distressing, because the old-fashioned conventional eye-rhymes are accepted as such without speech-adaptation, and to many ears are a pleasant relief from the fixed jingle of the perfect rhyme; whereas his false ear-rhymes ask to have their slight but indispensable differences obliterated in the reading, and thus they expose their defect, which is of a disagreeable and vulgar or even comic quality. He did not escape full criticism and ample ridicule for such things in his lifetime; and in '83 he wrote: "Some of my rhymes I regret, but they are past changing, grubs in amber: there are only a few of these; others are unassailable; some others again there are which malignity may munch at but the Muses love."

Now these are bad faults, and, as I said, a reader, if he is to get any enjoyment from the author's genius, must be somewhat tolerant of them; and they have a real relation to the means whereby the very forcible and original effects of beauty are produced. There is nothing stranger in these poems than the mixture of passages of extreme delicacy and exquisite diction with passages where, in a jungle of rough root-words, emphasis seems to oust euphony; and both these qualities, emphasis and euphony, appear in their extreme forms. It was an idiosyncrasy of this student's mind to push everything to its logical extreme, and take pleasure in a paradoxical result; as may be seen in his prosody where a simple theory seems to be used only as a basis for unexampled liberty. He was flattered when I called him, and saw the humour of it—and one would expect to find in his work the force of emphatic condensation and the magic of melodious expression, both in their extreme forms. Now since those who study style in itself must allow a proper place to the emphatic expression, this experiment, which supplies as novel examples of success as of failure, should be full of interest; and such interest will promote tolerance.

The fragment (see facsimiles a and b) is the draft of what appears to be an attempt to explain how an artist has not free-will in his creation. He works out his own nature instinctively as he happens to be made, and is irresponsible for the result. It is lamentable that Gerard Hopkins died when, to judge by his latest work, he was beginning to concentrate the force of all his luxuriant experiments in rhythm and diction, and castigate his art into a more reserved style. Few will read the terrible[39] posthumous sonnets without such high admiration and respect for his poetical power as must lead them to search out the rare masterly beauties that distinguish his work.

★ ★ ★

---

[39] Bridges uses this word in the sense of *inspiring fear or dread*.

~

Early Poems 1864–1866

~

Note by Robert Bridges

Two school prize-poems exist; the date of the first, "The Escorial," is Easter '60, which is before G. M. H. was sixteen years old. It is in Spenserian stanza: the imperfect copy in another hand has the first 15 stanzas omitting the 9th, and the author has written on it his motto:

Βάτραχος δέ ποτ' ἀκρίδας ὥς τις ἐρίσδω

with an accompanying gloss to explain his allusions. Though wholly lacking the Byronic flush it looks as if influenced by the historical descriptions in *Childe Harold,* and might provide a quotation for a tourist's guide to Spain. The history seems competent, and the artistic knowledge precocious.

Here for a sample is the seventh stanza:

> This was no classic temple order'd round
> With massy pillars of the Doric mood
> Broad-fluted, nor with shafts acanthus-crown'd,
> Pourtray'd along the frieze with Titan's brood
> That battled Gods for heaven; brilliant-hued,
> With golden fillets and rich blazonry,
> Wherein beneath the cornice, horsemen rode
> With form divine, a fiery chivalry—
> Triumph of airy grace and perfect harmony.

The second prize-poem, "A Vision of Mermaids," is dated Xmas '62. The autograph of this, which is preserved, is headed by a very elaborate circular pen-and-ink drawing, 6 inches in diameter,—a sunset sea-piece with rocks and formal groups of mermaidens, five or six together, singing as they stand (apparently) half-immersed in the shallows as described

> But most in a half-circle watch'd the sun, &c.

This poem is in 143 lines of heroics. It betrays the influence of Keats, and when I introduced the author to the public in Miles's book,[40] I quoted from it, thinking it useful to show that his difficult later style was not due to inability to excel in established forms. The poem is altogether above the standard of school-prizes. I reprint the extract here:

> Soon—as when Summer of his sister Spring
> Crushes and tears the rare enjewelling,
> And boasting "I have fairer things than these"
> Plashes amidst the billowy apple-trees
> His lusty hands, in gusts of scented wind
> Swirling out bloom till all the air is blind
> With rosy foam and pelting blossom and mists
> Of driving vermeil-rain; and, as he lists,
> The dainty onyx-coronals deflowers,
> A glorious wanton;—all the wrecks in showers
> Crowd down upon a stream, and jostling thick
> With bubbles bugle-eyed, struggle and stick
> On tangled shoals that bar the brook—a crowd
> Of filmy globes and rosy floating cloud:—
> So those Mermaidens crowded to my rock.

> ★ ★ ★ ★

> But most in a half-circle watch'd the sun;
> And a sweet sadness dwelt on every one;
> I knew not why,—but know that sadness dwells
> On Mermaids—whether that they ring the knells
> Of seamen whelm'd in chasms of the mid-main,
> As poets sing; or that it is a pain
> To know the dusk depths of the ponderous sea,
> The miles profound of solid green, and be
> With loath'd cold fishes, far from man—or what;—
> I know the sadness but the cause know not.

---

[40] Alfred Miles's *The Poets and Poetry of the Century* (1893).

Then they, thus ranged, gan make full plaintively
A piteous Siren sweetness on the sea,
Withouten instrument, or conch, or bell,
Or stretch'd chords tuneable on turtle's shell;
Only with utterance of sweet breath they sung
An antique chaunt and in an unknown tongue.
Now melting upward through the sloping scale
Swell'd the sweet strain to a melodious wail;
Now ringing clarion-clear to whence it rose
Slumber'd at last in one sweet, deep, heart-broken close.

1862–1868

After the relics of his school-poems follow the poems written when an undergraduate at Oxford, of which there are four in this book—Nos. 1, 2, 3, and 52, all dating about 1866. Of this period some ten or twelve autograph poems exist, the most successful being religious verses worked in Geo. Herbert's manner, and these, I think, have been printed: there are two sonnets in Italian form and Shakesperian mood (refused by *Cornhill Magazine*); the rest are attempts at lyrical poems, mostly sentimental aspects of death: one of them "Winter with the Gulf-stream" was published in *Once a Week,* and reprinted at least in part in some magazine: the autograph copy is dated Aug. 1871, but G. M. H. told me that he wrote it when he was at school; whence I guess that he altered it too much to allow of its early dating. The following is a specimen of his signature at this date:

1868–1875

After these last-mentioned poems there is a gap of silence which may be accounted for in his own words from a letter to R. W. D. Oct. 5, '78: "What (verses) I had written I burnt before I became a Jesuit (i.e. 1868) and resolved to write no more, as not belonging to my profession, unless it were by the wish of my superiors; so for seven years I wrote nothing but two or three little presentation pieces which occasion called for. But when in the winter of '75 the Deutschland was wrecked in the mouth of the Thames and five Franciscan nuns, exiles from Germany by the Falck Laws, aboard of her were drowned I was affected by the account and happening to say so to my rector he said that he wished some one would write a poem on the subject. On this hint I set to work and, though my hand was out at first, produced one. I had long had haunting my ear the echo of a new rhythm which now I realised on paper.... I do not say the idea is altogether new...but no one has professedly used it and made it the principle throughout, that I know of.... However, I had to mark the stresses...and a great many more oddnesses could not but dismay an editor's eye, so that when I offered it to our magazine *The Month*...they dared not print it."

Of the *two or three presentation pieces* here mentioned one is certainly the Marian verses "Rosa mystica," published in the *The Irish Monthly*, May '98, and again in Orby Shipley's *Carmina Mariana*, 2nd series, p. 183: the autograph exists.

Another is supposed to be the "Ad Mariam," printed in the *Stonyhurst Magazine*, Feb. '94. This is in five stanzas of eight lines, in direct and competent imitation of Swinburne: no autograph has been found; and, unless Father Hopkins's views of poetic form had been provisionally deranged or suspended, the verses can hardly be attributed to him without some impeachment of his sincerity; and that being altogether above suspicion, I would not yield to the rather strong presumption which their technical skill supplies in favour of his authorship. It is true that the "Rosa mystica" is somewhat in the same light lilting manner; but that was probably common to most of these festal verses, and "Rosa mystica" is not open to the positive objections of verbal criticism which would reject the "Ad Mariam." He never sent me any copy of either of these pieces, as he did of his severer Marian poems (Nos. 18 and 37), nor mentioned them as productions of his serious Muse. I do not find that in either class of these attempts he met with any appreciation at the time; it was after the publication of Miles's book in 1894 that his co-religionists began to recognize his possible merits, and their enthusiasm has not perhaps been always wise. It is natural that they should, as some of them openly state they do, prefer the poems that I am rejecting to those which I print; but this edition was undertaken in response to a demand that, both in England and America, has gradually grown up from the genuinely poetic interest felt in the poems which I have gradually introduced to the public:—that interest has been no doubt welcomed and accompanied by the applause of his particular religious associates, but since their purpose is alien to mine I regret that I am unable to indulge it; nor can I put aside the overruling objection that G. M. H. would not have wished these "little presentation pieces" to be set among his more serious artistic work. I do not think that they would please any one who is likely to be pleased with this book.[41]

1.[42]
For a Picture of St. Dorothea

I bear a basket lined with grass;
I am so light, I am so fair,
That men must wonder as I pass
And at the basket that I bear,
Where in a newly-drawn green litter
Sweet flowers I carry,—sweets for bitter.

Lilies I shew you, lilies none,
None in Caesar's gardens blow,—
And a quince in hand,—not one
Is set upon your boughs below;
Not set, because their buds not spring;
Spring not, 'cause world is wintering.

But these were found in the East and South
Where Winter is the clime forgot.—
The dewdrop on the larkspur's mouth
O should it then be quenched not?
In starry water-meads they drew
These drops: which be they? stars or dew?

---

[41] All of Hopkins's verse, from juvenilia to marginalia to multi-draft variations and crossed-out lines, have since been collected and published in various editions.

[42] Written when an exhibitioner at Balliol College. Contemporary autograph in A, and another almost identical in H, both undated. Text from A. This poem was afterwards expanded, shedding its relative pronouns, to 48 lines divided among three speakers, "an Angel, the protonotary Theophilus, (and) a Catechumen": the grace and charm of original lost:—there is an autograph in A and other copies exist. This was the first of the poems that I saw, and G. M. H. wrote it out for me (in 1866?). [Note by R. Bridges.]

Had she a quince in hand? Yet gaze:
Rather it is the sizing moon.
Lo, linked heavens with milky ways!
That was her larkspur row.—So soon?
Sphered so fast, sweet soul?—We see
Nor fruit, nor flowers, nor Dorothy.

2.[43]

Heaven–Haven

A nun takes the veil

I have desired to go
     Where springs not fail,
To fields where flies no sharp and sided hail
     And a few lilies blow.

And I have asked to be
     Where no storms come,
Where the green swell is in the havens dumb,
     And out of the swing of the sea.

3.[44]

The Habit of Perfection

Elected Silence, sing to me
And beat upon my whorlèd ear,
Pipe me to pastures still and be
The music that I care to hear.

Shape nothing, lips; be lovely-dumb:
It is the shut, the curfew sent
From there where all surrenders come
Which only makes you eloquent.

---

[43] Contemporary autograph, on same page with last, in H. Text is from a slightly
later autograph undated in A. The different copies vary. [Note by R. Bridges.]

[44] Two autographs in A; the earlier dated Jan. 18, 19, 1866. The second, which is
a good deal altered, is apparently of same date as text of No. 2. Text follows this
later version. Published in Miles. [Note by R. Bridges.]

Be shelled, eyes, with double dark
And find the uncreated light:
This ruck and reel which you remark
Coils, keeps, and teases simple sight.

Palate, the hutch of tasty lust,
Desire not to be rinsed with wine:
The can must be so sweet, the crust
So fresh that come in fasts divine!

Nostrils, your careless breath that spend
Upon the stir and keep of pride,
What relish shall the censers send
Along the sanctuary side!

O feel-of-primrose hands, O feet
That want the yield of plushy sward,
But you shall walk the golden street
And you unhouse and house the Lord.

And, Poverty, be thou the bride
And now the marriage feast begun,
And lily-coloured clothes provide
Your spouse not laboured-at nor spun.

★ ★

Poems of 1876–1889

4.[45]
The Wreck of the Deutschland

To the happy memory of five Franciscan Nuns exiles by the Falk Laws drowned between midnight and morning of Dec. 7th. 1875

Part the First

1

    Thou mastering me
  God! giver of breath and bread;
World's strand, sway of the sea;
  Lord of living and dead;

---

[45] Text from B, title from A (see description of B on p. xxvii). In "The Spirit of Man" the original first stanza is given from A, and varies; otherwise B was not much corrected. Another transcript, now at St. Aloysius' College, Glasgow, was made by Rev. F. Bacon after A but before the correction of B. This was collated for me by the Rev. Father Geoffrey Bliss, S.J., and gave one true reading. Its variants are distinguished by G in the notes to the poem. The labour spent on this great metrical experiment must have served to establish the poet's prosody and perhaps his diction: therefore the poem stands logically as well as chronologically in the front of his book, like a great dragon folded in the gate to forbid all entrance, and confident in his strength from past success. This editor advises the reader to circumvent him and attack him later in the rear; for he was himself shamefully worsted in a brave frontal assault, the more easily perhaps because both subject and treatment were distasteful to him. A good method of approach is to read stanza 16 aloud to a chance company. To the metrist and rhythmist the poem will be of interest from the first, and throughout. [Note by R. Bridges.]

Thou hast bound bones and veins in me,
    fastened me flesh,
  And after it almost unmade, what with dread,
Thy doing: and dost thou touch me afresh?
Over again I feel thy finger and find thee.

2

      I did say yes
     O at lightning and lashed rod;
   Thou heardst me truer than tongue confess
    Thy terror, O Christ, O God;
  Thou knowest the walls, altar and hour and night:
  The swoon of a heart that the sweep and the hurl of thee trod
    Hard down with a horror of height:
And the midriff astrain with leaning of,
    laced with fire of stress.

3

     The frown of his face
    Before me, the hurtle of hell
   Behind, where, where was a, where was a place?
    I whirled out wings that spell
  And fled with a fling of the heart to the heart of the Host.
  My heart, but you were dovewinged, I can tell,
    Carrier-witted, I am bold to boast,
To flash from the flame to the flame then,
    tower from the grace to the grace.

4

     I am soft sift
    In an hourglass—at the wall
   Fast, but mined with a motion, a drift,
    And it crowds and it combs to the fall;
  I steady as a water in a well, to a poise, to a pane,
  But roped with, always, all the way down from the tall
    Fells or flanks of the voel[46], a vein
Of the gospel proffer, a pressure, a principle, Christ's gift.

---

[46] Father Bliss tells me that the Voel is a mountain not far from St. Beuno's College in N. Wales, where the poem was written: and Dr. Henry Bradley that *moel* is primarily an adj. meaning *bald*: it becomes a fem. subst. meaning *bare hill*, and preceded by the article *y* becomes *voel*, in modern Welsh spelt *foel*. This accounts for its being written without initial capital, the word being used generically; and the meaning, obscured by *roped*, is that the well is fed by the trickles of water within the flanks of the mountains.—Both A and B read *planks* for *flanks*; G gives the correction. [Note by R. Bridges.]

5

       I kiss my hand
         To the stars, lovely-asunder
     Starlight, wafting him out of it; and
        Glow, glory in thunder;
   Kiss my hand to the dappled-with-damson west:
Since, tho' he is under the world's splendour and wonder,
    His mystery must be instressed, stressed;
For I greet him the days I meet him,
    and bless when I understand.

6

       Not out of his bliss
       Springs the stress felt
     Nor first from heaven (and few know this)
      Swings the stroke dealt—
Stroke and a stress that stars and storms deliver,
That guilt is hushed by, hearts are flushed by and melt—
    But it rides time like riding a river
(And here the faithful waver, the faithless fable and miss).

7

       It dates from day
      Of his going in Galilee;
    Warm-laid grave of a womb-life grey;
      Manger, maiden's knee;
The dense and the driven Passion, and frightful sweat;
Thence the discharge of it, there its swelling to be,
    Though felt before, though in high flood yet—
   What none would have known of it, only the heart,
    being hard at bay,

8

       Is out with it! Oh,
      We lash with the best or worst
    Word last! How a lush-kept plush-capped sloe
     Will, mouthed to flesh-burst,
     Gush!—flush the man, the being with it, sour or sweet,
Brim, in a flash, full!—Hither then, last or first,
    To hero of Calvary, Christ's feet—
Never ask if meaning it, wanting it, warned of it—men go.

9

> Be adored among men,
>   God, three-numberèd form;
>   Wring thy rebel, dogged in den,
>   Man's malice, with wrecking and storm.
>   Beyond saying sweet, past telling of tongue,
>   Thou art lightning and love, I found it, a winter and warm;
> Father and fondler of heart thou hast wrung:
>   Hast thy dark descending and most art merciful then.

10

> With an anvil-ding
>   And with fire in him forge thy will
>   Or rather, rather then, stealing as Spring
>   Through him, melt him but master him still:
>   Whether at once, as once at a crash Paul,
>   Or as Austin, a lingering-out sweet skill,
> Make mercy in all of us, out of us all
>   Mastery, but be adored, but be adored King.

PART THE SECOND

11

> "Some find me a sword; some
>   The flange and the rail; flame,
>   Fang, or flood" goes Death on drum,
>   And storms bugle his fame.
>   But wè dream we are rooted in earth—Dust!
>   Flesh falls within sight of us, we, though our flower the same,
> Wave with the meadow, forget that there must
>   The sour scythe cringe, and the blear share come.

12

> On Saturday sailed from Bremen,
>   American-outward-bound,
>   Take settler and seamen, tell men with women,
>   Two hundred souls in the round—
>   O Father, not under thy feathers nor ever as guessing
>   The goal was a shoal, of a fourth the doom to be drowned;
> Yet did the dark side of the bay of thy blessing
>   Not vault them, the million of rounds of thy mercy
>   not reeve even them in?

13

      Into the snows she sweeps,
        Hurling the haven behind,
    The Deutschland, on Sunday; and so the sky keeps,
        For the infinite air is unkind,
  And the sea flint-flake, black-backed in the regular blow,
  Sitting Eastnortheast, in cursed quarter, the wind;
    Wiry and white-fiery and whirlwind-swivellèd snow
Spins to the widow-making unchilding unfathering deeps.

14

      She drove in the dark to leeward,
        She struck—not a reef or a rock
    But the combs of a smother of sand: night drew her
        Dead to the Kentish Knock[47];
  And she beat the bank down with her bows and
  the ride of her keel:
  The breakers rolled on her beam with ruinous shock;
    And canvas and compass, the whorl and the wheel
Idle for ever to waft her or wind her with, these she endured.

15

      Hope had grown grey hairs,
        Hope had mourning on,
    Trenched with tears, carved with cares,
        Hope was twelve hours gone;
  And frightful a nightfall folded rueful a day
    Nor rescue, only rocket and lightship, shone,
  And lives at last were washing away:
To the shrouds they took,—they shook in the hurling
  and horrible airs.

16

      One stirred from the rigging to save
        The wild woman-kind below,
    With a rope's end round the man, handy and brave—
        He was pitched to his death at a blow,
  For all his dreadnought breast and braids of thew:
    They could tell him for hours, dandled the to and fro
  Through the cobbled foam-fleece, what could he do
With the burl of the fountains of air, buck and
  flood of the wave?

---

[47] *Kentish Knock:* a sandbar off the mouth of the Thames.

17

They fought with God's cold—
And they could not and fell to the deck
(Crushed them) or water (and drowned them) or rolled
With the sea-romp over the wreck.
Night roared, with the heart-break hearing
a heart-broke rabble,
The woman's wailing, the crying of child without check—
Till a lioness arose breasting the babble,
A prophetess towered in the tumult, a virginal tongue told.

18

Ah, touched in your bower of bone
Are you! turned for an exquisite smart,
Have you! make words break from me here all alone,
Do you!—mother of being in me, heart.
O unteachably after evil, but uttering truth,
Why, tears! is it? tears; such a melting, a madrigal start!
Never-eldering revel and river of youth,
What can it be, this glee? the good you have there of your own?

19

Sister, a sister calling
A master, her master and mine!—
And the inboard seas run swirling and hawling;
The rash smart sloggering brine
Blinds her; but she that weather sees one thing, one;
Has one fetch in her: she rears herself to divine
Ears, and the call of the tall nun
To the men in the tops and the tackle rode
over the storm's brawling.

20

She was first of a five and came
Of a coifèd sisterhood.
(O Deutschland, double a desperate name!
O world wide of its good!
But Gertrude, lily, and Luther, are two of a town,
Christ's lily and beast of the waste wood:
From life's dawn it is drawn down,
Abel is Cain's brother and breasts they have sucked the same.)

21

      Loathed for a love men knew in them,
        Banned by the land of their birth,
    Rhine refus1ed them. Thames would ruin them;
        Surf, snow, river and earth
   Gnashed: but thou art above, thou Orion of light;
   Thy unchancelling poising palms were weighing the worth,
        Thou martyr-master: in thy sight
Storm flakes were scroll-leaved flowers, lily showers—
   sweet heaven was astrew in them.

22

      Five! the finding and sake
        And cipher of suffering Christ.
     Mark, the mark is of man's make
        And the word of it Sacrificed.
   But he scores it in scarlet himself on his own bespoken,
     Before-time-taken, dearest prizèd and priced—
        Stigma, signal, cinquefoil token
For lettering of the lamb's fleece, ruddying of the rose-flake.

23

      Joy fall to thee, father Francis,
        Drawn to the Life that died;
    With the gnarls of the nails in thee, niche of the lance, his
        Lovescape crucified
   And seal of his seraph-arrival! and these thy daughters
   And five-livèd and leavèd favour and pride,
        Are sisterly sealed in wild waters,
To bathe in his fall-gold mercies,
   to breathe in his all-fire glances.

24

      Away in the loveable west,
        On a pastoral forehead of Wales,
    I was under a roof here, I was at rest,
        And they the prey of the gales;
   She to the black-about air, to the breaker, the thickly
   Falling flakes, to the throng that catches and quails,
        Was calling "O Christ, Christ come quickly":
The cross to her she calls Christ to her,
   christens her wild-worn Best.

25

> The majesty! what did she mean?
> Breathe, arch and original Breath.
> Is it love in her of the being as her lover had been?
> Breathe, body of lovely Death.
> They were else-minded then, altogether, the men
> Woke thee with a we are perishing in the weather
> of Gennesareth.
> Or is it that she cried for the crown then,
> The keener to come at the comfort for feeling
> the combating keen?

26

> For how to the heart's cheering
> The down-dugged ground-hugged grey
> Hovers off, the jay-blue heavens appearing
> Of pied and peeled May!
> Blue-beating and hoary-glow height; or night, still higher,
> With belled fire and the moth-soft Milky Way,
> What by your measure is the heaven of desire,
> The treasure never eyesight got, nor was ever guessed
> what for the hearing?

27

> No, but it was not these.
> The jading and jar of the cart,
> Time's tasking, it is fathers that asking for ease
> Of the sodden-with-its-sorrowing heart,
> Not danger, electrical horror; then further it finds
> The appealing of the Passion is tenderer in prayer apart:
> Other, I gather, in measure her mind's
> Burden, in wind's burly and beat of endragonèd seas.

28

> But how shall I...make me room there:
> Reach me a...Fancy, come faster—
> Strike you the sight of it? look at it loom there,
> Thing that she...there then! the Master,
> *Ipse*[48], the only one, Christ, King, Head:
> He was to cure the extremity where he had cast her;
> Do, deal, lord it with living and dead;
> Let him ride, her pride, in his triumph,
> despatch and have done with his doom there.

---

[48] *Ipse:* That is, He Himself.

29

        Ah! there was a heart right!
       There was single eye!
     Read the unshapeable shock night
      And knew the who and the why;
   Wording it how but by him that present and past,
   Heaven and earth are word of, worded by?—
     The Simon Peter of a soul! to the blast
 Tarpeian-fast, but a blown beacon of light.

30

        Jesu, heart's light,
       Jesu, maid's son,
     What was the feast followed the night
      Thou hadst glory of this nun?—
   Feast of the one woman without stain.
   For so conceivèd, so to conceive thee is done;
     But here was heart-throe, birth of a brain,
Word, that heard and kept thee and uttered thee outright.

31

       Well, she has thee for the pain, for the
      Patience; but pity of the rest of them!
     Heart, go and bleed at a bitterer vein for the
      Comfortless unconfessed of them—
   No not uncomforted: lovely-felicitous Providence
   Finger of a tender of, O of a feathery delicacy,
     the breast of the
   Maiden could obey so, be a bell to, ring of it, and
 Startle the poor sheep back! is the shipwrack then a harvest;
   does tempest carry the grain for thee?

32

       I admire thee, master of the tides,
      Of the Yore-flood, of the year's fall;
     The recurb and the recovery of the gulf's sides,
      The girth of it and the wharf of it and the wall;
   Stanching, quenching ocean of a motionable mind;
   Ground of being, and granite of it: past all
     Grasp God, throned behind
Death with a sovereignty that heeds but hides,
   bodes but abides;

33

      With a mercy that outrides
     The all of water, an ark
   For the listener; for the lingerer with a love glides
    Lower than death and the dark;
 A vein for the visiting of the past-prayer, pent in prison,
 The-last-breath penitent spirits—the uttermost mark
   Our passion-plungèd giant risen,
The Christ of the Father compassionate,
  fetched in the storm of his strides.

34

     Now burn, new born to the world,
    Doubled-naturèd name,
   The heaven-flung, heart-fleshed, maiden-furled
    Miracle-in-Mary-of-flame,
 Mid-numbered He in three of the thunder-throne!
 Not a dooms-day dazzle in his coming nor dark as he came;
   Kind, but royally reclaiming his own;
A released shower, let flash to the shire, not a lightning
 of fire hard-hurled.

35

     Dame, at our door
    Drowned, and among our shoals,
   Remember us in the roads, the heaven-haven
    of the Reward:
    Our King back, oh, upon English souls!
 Let him easter in us, be a dayspring to the dimness of us,
  be a crimson-cresseted east,
 More brightening her, rare-dear Britain, as his reign rolls,
   Pride, rose, prince, hero of us, high-priest,
Our hearts' charity's hearth's fire, our thoughts'
  chivalry's throng's Lord.

5.[49]
Penmaen Pool

For the Visitors' Book at the Inn

Who long for rest, who look for pleasure
Away from counter, court, or school
O where live well your lease of leisure
But here at, here at Penmaen Pool?

You'll dare the Alp? you'll dart the skiff?—
Each sport has here its tackle and tool:
Come, plant the staff by Cadair cliff;
Come, swing the sculls on Penmaen Pool.

What's yonder?—Grizzled Dyphwys dim:
The triple-hummocked Giant's stool,
Hoar messmate, hobs and nobs with him
To halve the bowl of Penmaen Pool.

And all the landscape under survey,
At tranquil turns, by nature's rule,
Rides repeated topsyturvy
In frank, in fairy Penmaen Pool.

And Charles's Wain, the wondrous seven,
And sheep-flock clouds like worlds of wool.
For all they shine so, high in heaven,
Shew brighter shaken in Penmaen Pool.

The Mawddach, how she trips! though throttled
If floodtide teeming thrills her full,
And mazy sands all water-wattled
Waylay her at ebb, past Penmaen Pool.

But what's to see in stormy weather,
When grey showers gather and gusts are cool?—
Why, raindrop-roundels looped together
That lace the face of Penmaen Pool.

---

[49] Early copy in A. Text, title, and punctuation from autograph in B, dated "Barmouth, Merionethshire. Aug. 1876." But that autograph writes *leisure* for *pleasure* in first line; skulls in stanza 2; and in stanza 8, *month* has a capital initial. Several copies exist, and vary. [Note by R. Bridges.]

Then even in weariest wintry hour
Of New Year's month or surly Yule
Furred snows, charged tuft above tuft, tower
From darksome darksome[50] Penmaen Pool.

And ever, if bound here hardest home,
You've parlour-pastime left and (who'll
Not honour[51] it?) ale like goldy foam
That frocks an oar in Penmaen Pool.

Then come who pine for peace or pleasure
Away from counter, court, or school,
Spend here your measure of time and treasure
And taste the treats of Penmaen Pool.

6.[52]
The Silver Jubilee:

To James First Bishop of Shrewsbury
on the 25th Year of his Episcopate July 28, 1876

1

Though no high-hung bells or din
Of braggart bugles cry it in—
    What is sound? Nature's round
Makes the Silver Jubilee.

2

Five and twenty years have run
Since sacred fountains to the sun
    Sprang, that but now were shut,
Showering Silver Jubilee.

3

Feasts, when we shall fall asleep,
Shrewsbury may see others keep;
    None but you this her true,
This her Silver Jubilee.

---

[50] Several variants. Two good copies read *darksome danksome*; but the early copy in A has *darksome darksome*, which B returns to. [Note by R. Bridges.]

[51] A has *But praise it*, and two good copies *But honour it*. [Note by R. Bridges.]

[52] "In honour of the Most Reverend James first Bishop of Shrewsbury. St. Beuno's, Vale of Clwyd. 1876, I think." A.—Text and title from autograph in B. It was published with somebody's sermon on the same occasion. Another copy in H. [Note by R. Bridges.]

4

> Not today we need lament
> Your wealth of life is some way spent:
>   Toil has shed round your head
> Silver but for Jubilee.

5

> Then for her whose velvet vales
> Should have pealed with welcome, Wales,
>   Let the chime of a rhyme
> Utter Silver Jubilee.

7.[53]
God's Grandeur

The world is charged with the grandeur of God.
   It will flame out, like shining from shook foil;
   It gathers to a greatness, like the ooze of oil
Crushed. Why do men then now not reck his rod?
Generations have trod, have trod, have trod;
   And all is seared with trade; bleared, smeared with toil;
   And wears man's smudge and shares man's smell: the soil
Is bare now, nor can foot feel, being shod.

And for all this, nature is never spent;
   There lives the dearest freshness deep down things;
And though the last lights off the black West went
   Oh, morning, at the brown brink eastward, springs—
Because the Holy Ghost over the bent
   World broods with warm breast and with ah! bright wings.

---

[53] "Standard rhythm counterpointed." Two autographs, Feb. 23, 1877; and March 1877; in A.—Text is from corrections in B. The second version in A has *lightning for shining* in line 2, explained in a letter of Jan. 4, '83. B returns to original word. [Note by R. Bridges.]

8.[54]
The Starlight Night

Look at the stars! look, look up at the skies!
   O look at all the fire-folk sitting in the air!
   The bright boroughs, the circle-citadels there!
Down in dim woods the diamond delves! the elves'-eyes!
The grey lawns cold where gold, where quickgold lies!
   Wind-beat whitebeam! airy abeles set on a flare!
   Flake-doves sent floating forth at a farmyard scare!—
Ah well! it is all a purchase, all is a prize.

Buy then! bid then!—What?—Prayer, patience, alms, vows.
Look, look: a May-mess, like on orchard boughs!
   Look! March-bloom, like on mealed-with-yellow sallows!
These are indeed the barn; withindoors house
The shocks. This piece-bright paling shuts the spouse
   Christ home, Christ and his mother and all his hallows.

9.[55]
Spring

Nothing is so beautiful as spring—
   When weeds, in wheels, shoot long and lovely and lush;
   Thrush's eggs look little low heavens, and thrush
Through the echoing timber does so rinse and wring
The ear, it strikes like lightnings to hear him sing;
   The glassy peartree leaves and blooms, they brush
   The descending blue; that blue is all in a rush
With richness; the racing lambs too have fair their fling.

---

[54] "Feb. 24, '77." Autograph in A.—"Standard rhythm opened and counterpointed. March '77." A.—Later corrected version "St. Beuno's, Feb. '77" in B.—Text follows B. The second version in A was published in Miles's book *Poets and Poetry of the Century.* [Note by R. Bridges.]

[55] "(Standard rhythm, opening with sprung leadings), May 1877." Autograph in A.—Text from corrections in B, but punctuation from A. Was published in Miles's book [*Poets and Poetry of the Century*] from incomplete correction of A. [Note by R. Bridges.]

What is all this juice and all this joy?
    A strain of the earth's sweet being in the beginning
In Eden garden.—Have, get, before it cloy,
    Before it cloud, Christ, lord, and sour with sinning,
Innocent mind and Mayday in girl and boy,
    Most, O maid's child, thy choice and worthy the winning.

10.[56]
The Lantern out of Doors

Sometimes a lantern moves along the night,
    That interests our eyes. And who goes there?
    I think; where from and bound, I wonder, where,
With, all down darkness wide, his wading light?

Men go by me whom either beauty bright
    In mould or mind or what not else makes rare:
    They rain against our much-thick and marsh air
Rich beams, till death or distance buys them quite.

Death or distance soon consumes them: wind
    What most I may eye after, be in at the end
I cannot, and out of sight is out of mind.

Christ minds: Christ's interest, what to avow or amend
    There, éyes them, heart wánts, care haúnts, foot fóllows kind,
Their ránsom, théir rescue, ánd first, fást, last friénd.

---

[56] "(Standard rhythm, with one sprung leading and one line counterpointed.)"
Autograph in A.— Text, title, and accents in lines 13 and 14, from corrections in B, where it is called "companion to No. 26, St. Beuno's '77."
[Note by R. Bridges.]

11.[57]
The Sea and the Skylark

On ear and ear two noises too old to end
   Trench—right, the tide that ramps against the shore;
   With a flood or a fall, low lull-off or all roar,
Frequenting there while moon shall wear and wend.

Left hand, off land, I hear the lark ascend,
   His rash-fresh re-winded new-skeinèd score
   In crisps of curl off wild winch whirl, and pour
And pelt music, till none's to spill nor spend.

How these two shame this shallow and frail town!
   How ring right out our sordid turbid time,
Being pure! We, life's pride and cared-for crown,

Have lost that cheer and charm of earth's past prime:
   Our make and making break, are breaking, down
To man's last dust, drain fast towards man's first slime.

---

[57] "Standard rhythm, in parts sprung and in others counterpointed, Rhyl, May '77." A. This version deleted in B, and the revision given in text written in with new title.—G. M. H. was not pleased with this sonnet, and wrote the following explanation of it in a letter '82: *"Rash fresh more* (it is dreadful to explain these things in cold blood) means a headlong and exciting new snatch of singing, resumption by the lark of his song, which by turns he gives over and takes up again all day long, and this goes on, the sonnet says, through all time, without ever losing its first freshness, being a thing both new and old. *Repair* means the same thing, renewal, resumption. The *skein* and *coil* are the lark's song, which from his height gives the impression of something falling to the earth and not vertically quite but tricklingly or wavingly, something as a skein of silk ribbed by having been tightly wound on a narrow card or a notched holder or as twine or fishing-tackle unwinding from a *reel* or *winch* or as pearls strung on a horsehair: the laps or folds are the notes or short measures and bars of them. The same is called a *score* in the musical sense of score and this score is 'writ upon a liquid sky trembling to welcome it,' only not horizontally. The lark in wild glee *races the reel round,* paying or dealing out and down the turns of the skein or *coil* right to the earth *floor,* the ground, where it lies in a heap, as it were, or rather is all wound off on to another winch, reel, bobbin or spool in Fancy's eye, by the moment the bird touches earth and so is ready for a fresh unwinding at the next flight. *Crisp* means almost *crisped,* namely with notes." [Note by R. Bridges.]

12.[58]
The Windhover:
To Christ our Lord

I caught this morning morning's minion, king-
    dom of daylight's dauphin, dapple-dawn-drawn Falcon, in his
      riding
Of the rolling level underneath him steady air, and striding
High there, how he rung upon the rein of a wimpling wing
In his ecstasy! then off, off forth on swing,
    As a skate's heel sweeps smooth on a bow-bend: the hurl and
      gliding
    Rebuffed the big wind. My heart in hiding
Stirred for a bird,—the achieve of, the mastery of the thing!

Brute beauty and valour and act, oh, air, pride, plume, here
    Buckle! AND the fire that breaks from thee then, a billion
Times told lovelier, more dangerous, O my chevalier!

    No wonder of it: shéer plód makes plough down sillion
Shine, and blue-bleak embers, ah my dear,
    Fall, gall themselves, and gash gold-vermillion.

13.[59]
Pied Beauty

Glory be to God for dappled things—
    For skies of couple-colour as a brinded cow;
      For rose-moles all in stipple upon trout that swim:
Fresh-firecoal chestnut-falls; finches' wings;
    Landscape plotted and pieced—fold, fallow, and plough;
      And áll trádes, their gear and tackle and trim.

---

[58] "(Falling paeonic rhythm, sprung and outriding.)" Two contemporary autographs in A.—Text and dedication from corrected B, dated St. Beuno's, May
30, 1877.—In a letter June 22, '79: "I shall shortly send you an amended copy
of 'The Windhover': the amendment only touches a single line, I think, but as
that is the best thing I ever wrote I should like you to have it in its best form."
[Note by R. Bridges.]

[59] "Curtal Sonnet: sprung paeonic rhythm. St. Beuno's, Tremeirchion. Summer
'77." Autograph in A.—B agrees. [Note by R. Bridges.]

All things counter, original, spare, strange;
   Whatever is fickle, freckled (who knows how?)
      With swift, slow; sweet, sour; adazzle, dim;
He fathers-forth whose beauty is past change:
     Praise him.

14.[60]
Hurrahing in Harvest

Summer ends now; now, barbarous in beauty, the stooks arise
   Around; up above, what wind-walks! what lovely behaviour
   Of silk-sack clouds! has wilder, wilful-wavier
Meal-drift moulded ever and melted across skies?

I walk, I lift up, I lift up heart, eyes,
   Down all that glory in the heavens to glean our Saviour;
   And, éyes, heárt, what looks, what lips yet gave you a
Rapturous love's greeting of realer, of rounder replies?

And the azurous hung hills are his world-wielding shoulder
   Majestic—as a stallion stalwart, very-violet-sweet!—
These things, these things were here and but the beholder
   Wanting; which two when they once meet,
The heart rears wings bold and bolder
   And hurls for him, O half hurls earth for him off under his feet.

---

[60] "Sonnet (sprung and outriding rhythm. Take notice that the outriding feet are
not to be confused with dactyls or paeons, though sometimes the line might be
scanned either way. The strong syllable in an outriding foot has always a great
stress and after the outrider follows a short pause. The paeon is easier and more
flowing). Vale of Clwyd, Sept. 1, 1877." Autograph in A. Text is from corrected B, punctuation of original A. In a letter '78 he wrote: "The Hurrahing
sonnet was the outcome of half an hour of extreme enthusiasm as I walked
home alone one day from fishing in the Elwy." A also notes "no counterpoint."
[Note by R. Bridges.]

15.[61]
The Caged Skylark

As a dare-gale skylark scanted in a dull cage
    Man's mounting spirit in his bone-house, mean house, dwells—
    That bird beyond the remembering his free fells;
This in drudgery, day-labouring-out life's age.

Though aloft on turf or perch or poor low stage,
    Both sing sometimes the sweetest, sweetest spells,
    Yet both droop deadly sómetimes in their cells
Or wring their barriers in bursts of fear or rage.

Not that the sweet-fowl, song-fowl, needs no rest—
Why, hear him, hear him babble and drop down to his nest,
    But his own nest, wild nest, no prison.

Man's spirit will be flesh-bound when found at best,
But uncumbered: meadow-down is not distressed
    For a rainbow footing it nor he for his bónes rísen.

16.[62]
In the Valley of the Elwy

    I remember a house where all were good
        To me, God knows, deserving no such thing:
        Comforting smell breathed at very entering,
    Fetched fresh, as I suppose, off some sweet wood.
    That cordial air made those kind people a hood
        All over, as a bevy of eggs the mothering wing
        Will, or mild nights the new morsels of spring:
    Why, it seemed of course; seemed of right it should.

---

[61] "(Falling paeonic rhythm, sprung and outriding.)" Autograph in A. Text from corrected B which dates St. Beuno's, 1877. In line 13 B writes *úncúmberèd*. [Note by R. Bridges.]

[62] "(Standard rhythm, sprung and counterpointed.)" Autograph in A. Text is from corrected B, which dates as contemporary with No. 15, adding "for the companion to this see" No. 35. [Note by R. Bridges.]

Lovely the woods, waters, meadows, combes, vales,
All the air things wear that build this world of Wales;
   Only the inmate does not correspond:
God, lover of souls, swaying considerate scales,
Complete thy creature dear O where it fails,
   Being mighty a master, being a father and fond.

17.[63]
The Loss of the Eurydice
Foundered March 24, 1878

1

The Eurydice—it concerned thee, O Lord:
Three hundred souls, O alas! on board,
   Some asleep unawakened, all un-
warned, eleven fathoms fallen

2

Where she foundered! One stroke
Felled and furled them, the hearts of oak!
   And flockbells off the aerial
Downs' forefalls beat to the burial.

3

For did she pride her, freighted fully, on
Bounden bales or a hoard of bullion?—
   Precious passing measure,
Lads and men her lade and treasure.

4

She had come from a cruise, training seamen—
Men, boldboys soon to be men:
   Must it, worst weather,
Blast bole and bloom together?

---

[63] A contemporary copy in A has this note: "Written in sprung rhythm, the third line has 3 beats, the rest 4. The scanning runs on without break to the end of the stanza, so that each stanza is rather one long line rhymed in passage than four lines with rhymes at the ends."—B has an autograph of the poem as it came to be corrected ('83 or after), without the above note and dated "Mount St. Mary, Derbyshire, Apr. '78."—Text follows B.—The injurious rhymes are partly explained in the old note. [Note by R. Bridges.]

5

No Atlantic squall overwrought her
Or rearing billow of the Biscay water:
    Home was hard at hand
And the blow bore from land.

6

And you were a liar, O blue March day.
Bright sun lanced fire in the heavenly bay;
    But what black Boreas wrecked her? he
Came equipped, deadly-electric,

7

A beetling baldbright cloud thorough England
Riding: there did storms not mingle? and
    Hailropes hustle and grind their
Heavengravel? wolfsnow, worlds of it, wind there?

8

Now Carisbrook keep goes under in gloom;
Now it overvaults Appledurcombe;
    Now near by Ventnor town
It hurls, hurls off Boniface Down.

9

Too proud, too proud, what a press she bore!
Royal, and all her royals wore.
    Sharp with her, shorten sail!
Too late; lost; gone with the gale.

10

This was that fell capsize,
As half she had righted and hoped to rise
    Death teeming in by her portholes
Raced down decks, round messes of mortals.

11

Then a lurch forward, frigate and men;
"All hands for themselves" the cry ran then;
    But she who had housed them thither
Was around them, bound them or wound them with her.

12

Marcus Hare, high her captain,
Kept to her—care-drowned and wrapped in
    Cheer's death, would follow
His charge through the champ-white water-in-a-wallow.

13

All under Channel to bury in a beach her
Cheeks: Right, rude of feature,
    He thought he heard say
"Her commander! and thou too, and thou this way."

14

It is even seen[64], time's something server,
In mankind's medley a duty-swerver,
    At downright "No or yes?"
Doffs all, drives full for righteousness.

15

Sydney Fletcher, Bristol-bred,
(Low lie his mates now on watery bed)
    Takes to the seas and snows
As sheer down the ship goes.

16

Now her afterdraught gullies him too down;
Now he wrings for breath with the deathgush brown;
    Till a lifebelt and God's will
Lend him a lift from the sea-swill.

17

Now he shoots short up to the round air;
Now he gasps, now he gazes everywhere;
    But his eye no cliff, no coast or
Mark makes in the rivelling snowstorm.

18

Him, after an hour of wintry waves,
A schooner sights, with another, and saves,
    And he boards her in Oh! such joy
He has lost count what came next, poor boy.—

19

They say who saw one sea-corpse cold
He was all of lovely manly mould,
    Every inch a tar,
Of the best we boast our sailors are.

---

[64] *It is even seen.* In a letter May 30, '78, he explains: "You mistake the sense of this
as I feared it would be mistaken. I believed Hare to be a brave and conscientious
man, what I say is that even those who seem unconscientious will act the right
part at a great push....About *mortholes* I wince a little." [Note by R. Bridges.]

20

> Look, foot to forelock, how all things suit! he
> Is strung by duty, is strained to beauty,
> And brown-as-dawning-skinned
> With brine and shine and whirling wind.

21

> O his nimble finger, his gnarled grip!
> Leagues, leagues of seamanship
> Slumber in these forsaken
> Bones, this sinew, and will not waken.

22

> He was but one like thousands more,
> Day and night I deplore
> My people and born own nation,
> Fast foundering own generation.

23

> I might let bygones be—our curse
> Of ruinous shrine no hand or, worse,
> Robbery's hand is busy to
> Dress, hoar-hallowèd shrines unvisited;

24

> Only the breathing temple and fleet
> Life, this wildworth blown so sweet,
> These daredeaths, ay this crew, in
> Unchrist, all rolled in ruin—

25

> Deeply surely I need to deplore it,
> Wondering why my master bore it,
> The riving off that race
> So at home, time was, to his truth and grace

26

> That a starlight-wender[65] of ours would say
> The marvellous Milk was Walsingham Way
> And one—but let be, let be:
> More, more than was will yet be.—

---

[65] *A starlight-wender,* i. e. The island was so Marian that the folk supposed the Milky Way was a fingerpost to guide pilgrims to the shrine of the Virgin at Walsingham. *And one,* that is Duns Scotus the champion of the Immaculate Conception. See Sonnet No. 20. [Note by R. Bridges.]

27

    O well wept[66], mother have lost son;
    Wept, wife; wept, sweetheart would be one:
        Though grief yield them no good
    Yet shed what tears sad truelove should.

28

    But to Christ lord of thunder
    Crouch; lay knee by earth low under:
        "Holiest, loveliest, bravest,
    Save my hero, O Hero savest.

29

    And the prayer thou hearst me making
    Have, at the awful overtaking,
        Heard; have heard and granted
    Grace that day grace was wanted."

30

    Not that hell knows redeeming,
    But for souls sunk in seeming
        Fresh, till doomfire burn all,
    Prayer shall fetch pity eternal.

18.[67]
The May Magnificat

    May is Mary's month, and I
    Muse at that and wonder why:
        Her feasts follow reason,
        Dated due to season—

    Candlemas, Lady Day;
    But the Lady Month, May,
        Why fasten that upon her,
        With a feasting in her honour?

---

[66] *Well wept.* Grammar is as in "Well hit! well run!" &c. The meaning "You do well to weep." [Note by R. Bridges.]

[67] "(Sprung rhythm, four stresses in each line of the first couplet, three in each of the second. Stonyhurst, May '78.)" Autograph in A.—Text from later autograph in B. He wrote to me: "A Maypiece in which I see little good but the freedom of the rhythm." In penult stanza *cuckoo-call* has its hyphen deleted in B, leaving the words separate. [Note by R. Bridges.]

Is it only its being brighter
Than the most are must delight her?
   Is it opportunest
   And flowers finds soonest?

Ask of her, the mighty mother:
Her reply puts this other
   Question: What is Spring?—
   Growth in every thing—

Flesh and fleece, fur and feather,
Grass and green world all together;
   Star-eyed strawberry-breasted
   Throstle above her nested

Cluster of bugle blue eggs thin
Forms and warms the life within;
   And bird and blossom swell
   In sod or sheath or shell.

All things rising, all things sizing
Mary sees, sympathising
   With that world of good,
   Nature's motherhood.

Their magnifying of each its kind
With delight calls to mind
   How she did in her stored
   Magnify the Lord.

Well but there was more than this:
Spring's universal bliss
   Much, had much to say
   To offering Mary May.

When drop-of-blood-and-foam-dapple
Bloom lights the orchard-apple
   And thicket and thorp are merry
   With silver-surfèd cherry

And azuring-over greybell makes
Wood banks and brakes wash wet like lakes
   And magic cuckoocall
   Caps, clears, and clinches all—

This ecstasy all through mothering earth
Tells Mary her mirth till Christ's birth
    To remember and exultation
    In God who was her salvation.

19.[68]
Binsey Poplars
felled 1879

My aspens dear, whose airy cages quelled,
Quelled or quenched in leaves the leaping sun,
All felled, felled, are all felled;
    Of a fresh and following folded rank
        Not spared, not one
        That dandled a sandalled
    Shadow that swam or sank
On meadow and river and wind-wandering weed-winding bank.

O if we but knew what we do
    When we delve or hew—
Hack and rack the growing green!
    Since country is so tender
To touch, her being só slender,
That, like this sleek and seeing ball
But a prick will make no eye at all,
Where we, even where we mean
        To mend her we end her,
When we hew or delve:
After-comers cannot guess the beauty been.
    Ten or twelve, only ten or twelve
        Strokes of havoc únselve
            The sweet especial scene,
        Rural scene, a rural scene,
        Sweet especial rural scene.

---

[68] "Felled 1879. Oxford, March 1879." Autograph in A. Text from B, which alters four places. l. 8 *weed-winding:* an early draft has *weed-wounden.* [Note by R. Bridges.]

20.[69]
Duns Scotus's Oxford

Towery city and branchy between towers;
Cuckoo-echoing, bell-swarmèd, lark-charmèd,
　　rook-racked, river-rounded;
The dapple-eared lily below thee; that country and town did
Once encounter in, here coped and poisèd powers;

Thou hast a base and brickish skirt there, sours
That neighbour-nature thy grey beauty is grounded
Best in; graceless growth, thou hast confounded
Rural rural keeping—folk, flocks, and flowers.

Yet ah! this air I gather and I release
He lived on; these weeds and waters, these walls are what
He haunted who of all men most sways my spirits to peace;

Of realty the rarest-veinèd unraveller; a not
Rivalled insight, be rival Italy or Greece;
Who fired France for Mary without spot.

---

[69] "Oxford, March 1879." Autograph in A. Copy in B agrees but dates 1878.
[Note by R. Bridges.]

21.[70]
Henry Purcell

The poet wishes well to the divine genius of Purcell and praises him that, whereas other musicians have given utterance to the moods of man's mind, he has, beyond that, uttered in notes the very make and species of man as created both in him and in all men generally.

Have fair fallen[71], O fair, fair have fallen, so dear
To me, so arch-especial a spirit as heaves in Henry Purcell,
An age is now since passed, since parted; with the reversal
Of the outward sentence low lays him, listed to a heresy, here.

Not mood in him nor meaning, proud fire or sacred fear,
Or love or pity or all that sweet notes not his might nursle:
It is the forgèd feature finds me; it is the rehearsal
Of own, of abrupt self there so thrusts on, so throngs the ear.

Let him oh! with his air of angels then lift me, lay me! only I'll
Have an eye to the sakes of him, quaint moonmarks,
    to his pelted plumage under
Wings: so some great stormfowl, whenever he has walked
    his while

The thunder-purple seabeach plumèd purple-of-thunder,
If a wuthering of his palmy snow-pinions scatter a colossal smile
Off him, but meaning motion fans fresh our wits with wonder.

---

[70] "(Alexandrine: six stresses to the line. Oxford, April 1879.)" Autograph in A with argument as printed. Copy in B is uncorrected except that it adds the word *fresh* in last line. [Note by R. Bridges.]

[71] " 'Have fair fallen.' *Have* is the sing. imperative (or optative if you like) of the past, a thing possible and actual both in logic and grammar, but naturally a rare one. As in the 2nd pers. we say 'Have done' or in making appointments 'Have had your dinner beforehand,' so one can say in the 3rd pers. not only 'Fair fall' of what is present or future but also 'Have fair fallen' of what is past. The same thought (which plays a great part in my own mind and action) is more clearly expressed in the last stanza but one of the *Eurydice,* where you remarked it." Letter to R. B., Feb. 3, '83. [Note by R. Bridges.]

22.[72]
Peace

When will you ever, Peace, wild wooddove, shy wings shut,
Your round me roaming end, and under be my boughs?
When, when, Peace, will you, Peace? I'll not play hypocrite
To own my heart: I yield you do come sometimes; but
That piecemeal peace is poor peace. What pure peace allows
Alarms of wars, the daunting wars, the death of it?

O surely, reaving Peace, my Lord should leave in lieu
Some good! And so he does leave Patience exquisite,
That plumes to Peace thereafter. And when Peace here does house
He comes with work to do, he does not come to coo,
   He comes to brood and sit.

23.[73]
The Bugler's First Communion

A bugler boy from barrack (it is over the hill
There)—boy bugler, born, he tells me, of Irish
   Mother to an English sire (he
Shares their best gifts surely, fall how things will),

This very very day came down to us after a boon he on
My late being there begged of me, overflowing
   Boon in my bestowing,
Came, I say, this day to it—to a First Communion.

Here he knelt then ín regimental red.
Forth Christ from cupboard fetched, how fain I of feet
   To his youngster take his treat!
Low-latched in leaf-light housel his too huge godhead.

---

[72] "Oxford, 1879." Autograph in B, where a comma after *daunting* is due to following a deletion. T*o own my heart=to my own heart. Reaving Peace,* i.e. when he reaves or takes Peace away, as No. 35, l. 12. An early draft dated Oct. 2, '79, has *taking* for *reaving.* [Note by R. Bridges.]

[73] "(Sprung rhythm, overrove, an outride between the 3rd and 4th foot of the 4th line in each stanza.) Oxford, July 27, (?) 1879." A.—My copy of this in B shows three emendations. First draft exists in H. Text is A with the corrections from B. At nine lines from end, *Though this,* A has *Now this,* and *Now* is deliberately preferred in H.—B has some uncorrected miscopyings of A. *O for, now, charms* of A is already a correction in H. I should like a comma at end of first line of 5th stanza and an interjection-mark at end of that stanza. [Note by R. Bridges.]

There! and your sweetest sendings, ah divine,
By it, heavens, befall him! as a heart Christ's darling, dauntless;
   Tongue true, vaunt- and tauntless;
Breathing bloom of a chastity in mansex fine.

Frowning and forefending angel-warder
Squander the hell-rook ranks sally to molest him;
   March, kind comrade, abreast him;
Dress his days to a dexterous and starlight order.

How it dóes my heart good, visiting at that bleak hill,
When limber liquid youth, that to all I teach
   Yields tender as a pushed peach,
Hies headstrong to its wellbeing of a self-wise self-will!

Then though I should tread tufts of consolation
Dáys áfter, só I in a sort deserve to
   And do serve God to serve to
Just such slips of soldiery Christ's royal ration.

Nothing élse is like it, no, not all so strains
Us: fresh youth fretted in a bloomfall all portending
   That sweet's sweeter ending;
Realm both Christ is heir to and thére réigns.

O now well work that sealing sacred ointment!
O for now charms, arms, what bans off bad
   And locks love ever in a lad!
Let mé though see no more of him, and not disappointment

Those sweet hopes quell whose least me quickenings lift,
In scarlet or somewhere of some day seeing
   That brow and bead of being,
An our day's God's own Galahad. Though this child's drift

Seems by a divíne doom chánnelled, nor do I cry
Disaster there; but may he not rankle and roam
   In backwheels though bound home?—
That left to the Lord of the Eucharist, I here lie by;

Recorded only, I have put my lips on pleas
Would brandle adamantine heaven with ride and jar, did
   Prayer go disregarded:
Forward-like, but however, and like favourable heaven heard these.

24.[74]

Morning Midday and Evening Sacrifice

The dappled die-away
Cheek and wimpled lip,
The gold-wisp, the airy-grey
Eye, all in fellowship—
This, all this beauty blooming,
This, all this freshness fuming,
Give God while worth consuming.

Both thought and thew now bolder
And told by Nature: Tower;
Head, heart, hand, heel, and shoulder
That beat and breathe in power—
This pride of prime's enjoyment
Take as for tool, not toy meant
And hold at Christ's employment.

The vault and scope and schooling
And mastery in the mind,
In silk-ash kept from cooling,
And ripest under rind—
What life half lifts the latch of,
What hell stalks towards the snatch of,
Your offering, with despatch, of!

---

[74] "Oxford, Aug. '79." Autograph in A. The first stanza reproduced after p. 70. Copied by me into B, where it received correction. Text follows B except in lines 19 and 20, where the correction reads *What Death half lifts the latch of, What hell hopes soon the snatch of.* And punctuation is not all followed: original has comma after the second *this* in lines 5 and 6. On June 30, '86, G. M. H. wrote to Canon Dixon, who wished to print the first stanza alone in some anthology, and made *ad hoc* alterations which I do not follow. The original 17th line was *Silk-ashed but core not cooling,* and was altered because of its obscurity. "I meant (he wrote) to compare grey hairs to the flakes of silky ash which may be seen round wood embers... and covering a core of heat...." *Your offering, with despatch, of* is said like "your ticket," "your reasons," "your money or your life..." It is: "Come, your offer of all this (the matured mind), and without delay either!" [Note by R. Bridges.]

25.[75]
Andromeda

Now Time's Andromeda on this rock rude,
With not her either beauty's equal or
Her injury's, looks off by both horns of shore,
Her flower, her piece of being, doomed dragon's food.
  Time past she has been attempted and pursued
By many blows and banes; but now hears roar
A wilder beast from West than all were, more
Rife in her wrongs, more lawless, and more lewd.

  Her Perseus linger and leave her tó her extremes?—
Pillowy air he treads a time and hangs
His thoughts on her, forsaken that she seems,
  All while her patience, morselled into pangs,
Mounts; then to alight disarming, no one dreams,
With Gorgon's gear and barebill, thongs and fangs.

26.[76]
The Candle Indoors

Some candle clear burns somewhere I come by.
I muse at how its being puts blissful back
With yellowy moisture mild night's blear-all black,
Or to-fro tender trambeams truckle at the eye.

---

[75] "Oxford, Aug. 12, '79." A—which B corrects in two places only. Text rejects the first, in line 4 *dragon* for *dragon's:* but follows B in line 10, where A had *Air, pillowy air.* There is no comma at *barebill* in any MS., but a gap and sort of caesural mark in A. In a letter Aug. 14, '79, G. M. H. writes: "I enclose a sonnet on which I invite minute criticism. I endeavoured in it at a more Miltonic plainness and severity than I have anywhere else. I cannot say it has turned out severe, still less plain, but it seems almost free from quaintness and in aiming at one excellence I may have hit another." [Note by R. Bridges.]

[76] "(Common rhythm, counterpointed.) Oxford, '79." A. Text takes corrections of B, which adds "companion to" No. 10. A has in line 2 *With a yellowy,* and 5 *At that.* [Note by R. Bridges.]

By that window what task what fingers ply,
I plod wondering, a-wanting, just for lack
Of answer the eagerer a-wanting Jessy or Jack
There / God to aggrándise, God to glorify.—[77]

Come you indoors, come home; your fading fire
Mend first and vital candle in close heart's vault:
You there are master, do your own desire;
What hinders? Are you beam-blind, yet to a fault
In a neighbour deft-handed? Are you that liar
And, cast by conscience out, spendsavour salt?

27.[78]
The Handsome Heart:
at a Gracious Answer

"But tell me, child, your choice; what shall I buy
You?"—"Father, what you buy me I like best."
With the sweetest air that said, still plied and pressed,
He swung to his first poised purport of reply.

What the heart is! which, like carriers let fly—
Doff darkness, homing nature knows the rest—
To its own fine function, wild and self-instressed,
Falls light as ten years long taught how to and why.

Mannerly-hearted! more than handsome face—
Beauty's bearing or muse of mounting vein,
All, in this case, bathed in high hallowing grace...

---

[77] *There /...:* the oblique slash denotes a pause after the enjambment of "There," and also gives space and stress to "God." [Note by Thomas Crofts. *God's Grandeur and Other Poems.* New York: Dover. 1995.]

[78] "(Common rhythm counterpointed.) Oxford, '79." A₁.—In Aug. of the same year he wrote that he was surprised at my liking it, and in deference to my criticism sent a revise, A₂.—Subsequently he recast the sonnet mostly in the longer 6-stress lines, and wrote that into B.—In that final version the charm and freshness have disappeared: and his emendation in evading the clash of *ply* and *reply* is awkward; also the fourteen lines now contain seven *whats.* I have therefore taken A₁ for the text, and have ventured, in line 8, to restore *how to,* in the place of *what,* from the original version which exists in H. In "The Spirit of Man" I gave a mixture of A₁ and A₂. In line 5 the word *soul* is in H and A₁: but A₂ and B have *heart. Father* in second line was the Rev. Father Gerard himself. He tells the whole story in a letter to me. [Note by R. Bridges.]

Of heaven what boon to buy you, boy, or gain
Not granted?—Only...O on that path you pace
Run all your race, O brace sterner that strain!

28.[79]
At the Wedding March

God with honour hang your head,
Groom, and grace you, bride, your bed
With lissome scions, sweet scions,
Out of hallowed bodies bred.

Each be other's comfort kind:
Déep, déeper than divined,
Divine charity, dear charity,
Fast you ever, fast bind.

Then let the March tread our ears:
I to him turn with tears
Who to wedlock, his wonder wedlock,
Déals tríumph and immortal years.

29.[80]
Felix Randal

Felix Randal the farrier, O he is dead then? my duty all ended,
Who have watched his mould of man, big-boned
    and hardy-handsome
Pining, pining, till time when reason rambled in it and some
Fatal four disorders, fleshed there, all contended?

Sickness broke him. Impatient he cursed at first, but mended
Being anointed and all; though a heavenlier heart began some
Months earlier, since I had our sweet reprieve and ransom
Tendered to him. Ah well, God rest him all road ever he offended!

---

[79] "(Sprung rhythm.) Bedford, Lancashire, Oct. 21, '79." A. Autograph uncorrected
in B, but title changed to that in text. [Note by R. Bridges.]

[80] "(Sonnet: sprung and outriding rhythm; six-foot lines.) Liverpool, Apr. 28, '80."
A. Text from A with the two corrections of B. The comma in line 5 after *impatient*
is omitted in copy in B. [Note by R. Bridges.]

This seeing the sick endears them to us, us too it endears.
My tongue had taught thee comfort, touch had quenched thy tears,
Thy tears that touched my heart, child, Felix, poor Felix Randal;

How far from then forethought of, all thy more boisterous years,
When thou at the random grim forge, powerful amidst peers,
Didst fettle for the great grey drayhorse his bright
    and battering sandal!

30.[81]
Brothers

How lovely the elder brother's
Life all laced in the other's,
Lóve-laced! what once I well
Witnessed; so fortune fell.
When Shrovetide, two years gone,
Our boys' plays brought on
Part was picked for John,
Young Jóhn: then fear, then joy
Ran revel in the elder boy.
Their night was come now; all
Our company thronged the hall;
Henry, by the wall,
Beckoned me beside him:
I came where called, and eyed him
By meanwhiles; making mý play
Turn most on tender byplay.
For, wrung all on love's rack,
My lad, and lost in Jack,
Smiled, blushed, and bit his lip;
Or drove, with a diver's dip,
Clutched hands down through clasped knees—

---

[81] "(Sprung rhythm; three feet to the line; lines free-ended and not overrove; and
reversed or counterpointed rhythm allowed in the first foot.) Hampstead, Aug.
1880." Five various drafts exist. A$_1$ and A$_2$ both of Aug. '80. B was copied by
me from A$_1$, and author's emendations of it overlook those in A$_2$. Text therefore
is from A$_2$ except that the first seven lines, being rewritten in margin afresh
(and confirmed in letter of Ap. '81 to Canon Dixon), as also corrections in
lines 15–18, these are taken. But the B corrections of lines 22, 23, almost certainly imply forgetfulness of A$_2$. In last line B has correction *Dearly thou canst be
kind;* but the intention of *I'll cry* was original, and has four MSS. in its favour.
[Note by R. Bridges.]

Truth's tokens tricks like these,
Old telltales, with what stress
He hung on the imp's success.
Now the other was bráss-bóld:
Hé had no work to hold
His heart up at the strain;
Nay, roguish ran the vein.
Two tedious acts were past;
Jack's call and cue at last;
When Henry, heart-forsook,
Dropped eyes and dared not look.
Eh, how áll rúng!
Young dog, he did give tongue!
But Harry—in his hands he has flung
His tear-tricked cheeks of flame
For fond love and for shame.
   Ah Nature, framed in fault,
There 's comfort then, there 's salt;
Nature, bad, base, and blind,
Dearly thou canst be kind;
There dearly thén, déarly,
I'll cry thou canst be kind.

31.[82]
Spring and Fall:
to a young child

Márgarét, are you gríeving
Over Goldengrove unleaving?
Leáves, líke the things of man, you
With your fresh thoughts care for, can you?
Áh! ás the heart grows older
It will come to such sights colder
By and by, nor spare a sigh
Though worlds of wanwood leafmeal lie;
And yet you wíll weep and know why.
Now no matter, child, the name:
Sórrow's spríngs áre the same.

---

[82] "(Sprung rhythm.) Lydiate, Lancashire, Sept. 7, 1880." A. Text and title from B, which corrects four lines, and misdates '81. There is also a copy in D, Jan. '81, and see again Apr. 6, '81. In line 2 the last word is *unleafing* in most of the MSS. An attempt to amend the second rhyme was unsuccessful. [Note by R. Bridges.]

Nor mouth had, no nor mind, expressed
What heart heard of, ghost guessed:
It ís the blight man was born for,
It is Margaret you mourn for.

32.[83]
Spelt from Sibyl's Leaves

Earnest, earthless, equal, attuneable, |
   vaulty, voluminous,…stupendous
Evening strains to be tíme's vást, |
   womb-of-all, home-of-all, hearse-of-all night.
Her fond yellow hornlight wound to the west, |
   her wild hollow hoarlight hung to the height
Waste; her earliest stars, earl-stars, | stárs principal, overbend us,
Fire-féaturing heaven. For earth |
   her being has unbound, her dapple is at an end, as-
tray or aswarm, all throughther, in throngs; |
   self ín self steepèd and páshed—quíte
Disremembering, dísmémbering |
   áll now. Heart, you round me right
With: Óur évening is over us; óur night |
   whélms, whélms, ánd will end us.
Only the beak-leaved boughs dragonish |
   damask the tool-smooth bleak light; black,
Ever so black on it. Óur tale, óur oracle! |
   Lét life, wáned, ah lét life wind
Off hér once skéined stained véined varíety |
   upon, áll on twó spools; párt, pen, páck
Now her áll in twó flocks, twó folds—black, white; |
   right, wrong; reckon but, reck but, mind

---

[83] "(Sonnet: sprung rhythm: a rest of one stress in the first line.)" Autograph in A—another later in B, which is taken for text. Date unrecorded. Lines 5, 6, *astray* thus divided to show the rhyme.—6. *throughther*, an adj., now confined to dialect. It is the speech form of *through-other*, in which shape it eludes pursuit in the Oxford dictionary. Dr. Murray compares Ger. *durch einander*. Mr. Craigie tells me that the classical quotation for it is from Burns's "Halloween," st. 5, *They roar an' cry a' throughther.*—line 8. *With,* i.e. I suppose, *with your warning that, &c.*: the heart is speaking.—9. *beak-leaved* is not hyphened in MS.—11. *part, pen, pack,* imperatives of the verbs, in the sense of sorting "the sheep from the goats."—12. A has *wrong right,* but the correction to *right wrong* in B is intentional.—14. *sheathe-* in both MSS., but I can only make sense of *sheath-,* i.e. "sheathless and shelterless." The accents in this poem are a selection from A and B. [Note by R. Bridges.]

But thése two; wáre of a wórld where bút these |
   twó tell, each off the óther; of a rack
Where, selfwrung, selfstrung, sheathe- and shelterless, |
   thóughts agaínst thoughts ín groans grínd.

33.[84]
Inversnaid

This darksome burn, horseback brown,
His rollrock highroad roaring down,
In coop and in comb the fleece of his foam
Flutes and low to the lake falls home.

A windpuff-bonnet of fáwn-fróth
Turns and twindles over the broth
Of a pool so pitchblack, féll-frówning,
It rounds and rounds Despair to drowning.

Degged with dew, dappled with dew
Are the groins of the braes that the brook treads through,
Wiry heathpacks, flitches of fern,
And the beadbonny ash that sits over the burn.

What would the world be, once bereft
Of wet and of wildness? Let them be left,
O let them be left, wildness and wet;
Long live the weeds and the wilderness yet.

---

[84] "Sept. 28, 1881." Autograph in H. I have found no other trace of this poem.
   [Note by R. Bridges.]

34.[85]
"As kingfishers catch fire..."

As kingfishers catch fire, dragonflies dráw fláme;
As tumbled over rim in roundy wells
Stones ring; like each tucked string tells, each hung bell's
Bow swung finds tongue to fling out broad its name;
Each mortal thing does one thing and the same:
Deals out that being indoors each one dwells;
Selves—goes itself; *myself* it speaks and spells,
Crying *Whát I do is me: for that I came.*

Í say móre: the just man justices;
Kéeps gráce: thát keeps all his goings graces;
Acts in God's eye what in God's eye he is—
Chríst—for Christ plays in ten thousand places,
Lovely in limbs, and lovely in eyes not his
To the Father through the features of men's faces.

35.[86]
Ribblesdale

Earth, sweet Earth, sweet landscape, with leavès throng
And louchèd low grass, heaven that dost appeal
To, with no tongue to plead, no heart to feel;
That canst but only be, but dost that long—

---

[85] Text from undated autograph in H, a draft with corrections and variants. In lines 3 and 4 *hung* and *to fling out broad* are corrections in same later pencilling as line 5, which occurs only thus with them. In sestet the first three lines have alternatives of regular rhythm, thus:

   Then I say more: the just man justices;

   Keeps grace and that keeps all his goings graces;

   In God's eye acts, &c.

Of these lines, in 9 and 10 the version given in text is later than the regular lines just quoted, and probably preferred: in l. 11 the alternatives apparently of same date. [Note by R. Bridges.]

[86] "Stonyhurst, 1882." Autograph in A. Text from later autograph in B, which adds "companion to No. 10" (=16). There is a third autograph in D, June '83 with different punctuation which gives the comma between *to* and *with* in line 3. The dash after *man* is from A and D, both of which quote "Nam expectatio cresturæ" &c. from Romans viii. 19. In the letter to R. W. D. he writes: *"Louched* is a coinage of mine, and is to mean much the same as slouched, slouching, and I mean *throng* for an adjective as we use it in Lancashire." But *louch* has ample authority, see the English Dialect Dictionary. [Note by R. Bridges.]

Thou canst but be, but that thou well dost; strong
Thy plea with him who dealt, nay does now deal,
Thy lovely dale down thus and thus bids reel
Thy river, and o'er gives all to rack or wrong.

And what is Earth's eye, tongue, or heart else, where
Else, but in dear and dogged man?—Ah, the heir
To his own selfbent so bound, so tied to his turn,
To thriftless reave both our rich round world bare
And none reck of world after, this bids wear
Earth brows of such care, care and dear concern.

36.[87]

The Leaden Echo and the Golden Echo
(Maidens' song from St. Winefred's Well)

THE LEADEN ECHO:

How to kéep—is there ány any, is there none such, nowhere
   known some, bow or brooch or braid or brace, láce,
   latch or catch or key to keep
Back beauty, keep it, beauty, beauty, beauty,…from vanishing away?
Ó is there no frowning of these wrinkles, rankèd wrinkles deep,
Dówn? no waving off of these most mournful messengers,
   still messengers, sad and stealing messengers of grey?
No there's none, there's none, O no there's none,
Nor can you long be, what you now are, called fair,
Do what you may do, what, do what you may,
And wisdom is early to despair:
Be beginning; since, no, nothing can be done
To keep at bay

---

[87] "Stonyhurst, Oct 13, '82." Autograph in A. Copy of this with autograph corrections dated Hampstead '81 *(sic)* in B.—Text takes all B's corrections, but respects punctuation of A, except that I have added the comma after *God* in line 26 of *The Golden Echo.* For the drama of *Winefred,* see among posthumous fragments, No. 58. In Nov. 1882 he wrote to me: "I am somewhat dismayed about that piece and have laid it aside for a while. I cannot satisfy myself about the first line. You must know that words like *charm* and *enchantment* will not do: the thought is of beauty as of something that can be physically kept and lost and by physical things only, like keys; then the things must come from the *mundus muliebris;* and thirdly they must not be markedly oldfashioned. You will see that this limits the choice of words very much indeed. However I shall make some changes. *Back* is not pretty, but it gives that feeling of physical constraint which I want." And in Oct. '86 to R. W. D., "I never did anything more musical." [Note by R. Bridges.]

Age and age's evils, hoar hair,
Ruck and wrinkle, drooping, dying, death's worst, winding sheets,
    tombs and worms and tumbling to decay;
So be beginning, be beginning to despair.
O there's none; no no no there's none:
Be beginning to despair, to despair,
Despair, despair, despair, despair.

THE GOLDEN ECHO:

          Spare!
There ís one, yes I have one (Hush there!);
Only not within seeing of the sun,
Not within the singeing of the strong sun,
Tall sun's tingeing, or treacherous the tainting of the earth's air.
Somewhere elsewhere there is ah well where! one,
One. Yes I can tell such a key, I do know such a place,
Where whatever's prized and passes of us, everything that's
    fresh and fast flying of us, seems to us sweet of us and
    swiftly away with, done away with, undone,
Undone, done with, soon done with, and yet dearly
    and dangerously sweet
Of us, the wimpled-water-dimpled, not-by-morning-matchèd face,
The flower of beauty, fleece of beauty, too too apt to, ah! to fleet,
Never fleets móre, fastened with the tenderest truth
To its own best being and its loveliness of youth: it is an
    ever-lastingness of, O it is an all youth!
Come then, your ways and airs and looks, locks, maiden gear,
    gallantry and gaiety and grace,
Winning ways, airs innocent, maiden manners, sweet looks, loose
    locks, long locks, lovelocks, gaygear, going gallant, girlgrace—
Resign them, sign them, seal them, send them, motion
    them with breath,
And with sighs soaring, soaring sighs deliver
Them; beauty-in-the-ghost, deliver it, early now, long before death
Give beauty back, beauty, beauty, beauty, back to God,
    beauty's self and beauty's giver.
See; not a hair is, not an eyelash, not the least lash lost; every hair
Is, hair of the head, numbered.
Nay, what we had lighthanded left in surly the mere mould
Will have waked and have waxed and have walked with the
    wind what while we slept,
This side, that side hurling a heavyheaded hundredfold
What while we, while we slumbered.

O then, weary then why should we tread? O why are we so haggard
   at the heart, so care-coiled, care-killed, so fagged, so fashed,
   so cogged, so cumbered,
When the thing we freely fórfeit is kept with fonder a care,
Fonder a care kept than we could have kept it, kept
Far with fonder a care (and we, we should have lost it) finer, fonder
A care kept.—Where kept? Do but tell us where kept, where.—
Yonder.—What high as that! We follow, now we follow.—
   Yonder, yes yonder, yonder,
Yonder.

37.[88]

The Blessed Virgin compared to the Air we Breathe

> Wild air, world-mothering air,
> Nestling me everywhere,
> That each eyelash or hair
> Girdles; goes home betwixt
> The fleeciest, frailest-flixed
> Snowflake; that's fairly mixed
> With, riddles, and is rife
> In every least thing's life;
> This needful, never spent,
> And nursing element;
> My more than meat and drink,
> My meal at every wink;
> This air, which, by life's law,
> My lung must draw and draw
> Now but to breathe its praise,
> Minds me in many ways
> Of her who not only
> Gave God's infinity
> Dwindled to infancy
> Welcome in womb and breast,
> Birth, milk, and all the rest

---

[88] "Stonyhurst, May '83." Autograph in A.—Text and title from later autograph in
B. Taken by Dean Beeching into *A Book of Christmas Verse*, 1895, and thence,
incorrectly, by Orby Shipley in *Carmina Mariana*. Stated in a letter to R. W. D.
June 25, '83, to have been written to "hang up among the verse compositions in
the tongues....I did a piece in the same metre as *Blue in the mists all day*." Note
Chaucer's account of the physical properties of the air, *House of Fame*, ii. 256, seq.
[Note by R. Bridges.]

But mothers each new grace
That does now reach our race—
Mary Immaculate,
Merely a woman, yet
Whose presence, power is
Great as no goddess's
Was deemèd, dreamèd; who
This one work has to do—
Let all God's glory through,
God's glory which would go
Through her and from her flow
Off, and no way but so.

    I say that we are wound
With mercy round and round
As if with air: the same
Is Mary, more by name.
She, wild web, wondrous robe,
Mantles the guilty globe,
Since God has let dispense
Her prayers his providence:
Nay, more than almoner,
The sweet alms' self is her
And men are meant to share
Her life as life does air.
    If I have understood,
She holds high motherhood
Towards all our ghostly good
And plays in grace her part
About man's beating heart,
Laying, like air's fine flood,
The deathdance in his blood;
Yet no part but what will
Be Christ our Saviour still.
Of her flesh he took flesh:
He does take fresh and fresh,
Though much the mystery how,
Not flesh but spirit now
And makes, O marvellous!
New Nazareths in us,
Where she shall yet conceive
Him, morning, noon, and eve;
New Bethlems, and he born
There, evening, noon, and morn—

Bethlem or Nazareth,
Men here may draw like breath
More Christ and baffle death;
Who, born so, comes to be
New self and nobler me
In each one and each one
More makes, when all is done,
Both God's and Mary's Son.
    Again, look overhead
How air is azurèd;
O how! nay do but stand
Where you can lift your hand
Skywards: rich, rich it laps
Round the four fingergaps.
Yet such a sapphire-shot,
Charged, steepèd sky will not
Stain light. Yea, mark you this:
It does no prejudice.
The glass-blue days are those
When every colour glows,
Each shape and shadow shows.
Blue be it: this blue heaven
The seven or seven times seven
Hued sunbeam will transmit
Perfect, not alter it.
Or if there does some soft,
On things aloof, aloft,
Bloom breathe, that one breath more
Earth is the fairer for.
Whereas did air not make
This bath of blue and slake
His fire, the sun would shake,
A blear and blinding ball
With blackness bound, and all
The thick stars round him roll
Flashing like flecks of coal,
Quartz-fret, or sparks of salt,
In grimy vasty vault.
    So God was god of old:
A mother came to mould
Those limbs like ours which are
What must make our daystar
Much dearer to mankind;

Whose glory bare would blind
Or less would win man's mind.
Through her we may see him
Made sweeter, not made dim,
And her hand leaves his light
Sifted to suit our sight.

    Be thou then, O thou dear
Mother, my atmosphere;
My happier world, wherein
To wend and meet no sin;
Above me, round me lie
Fronting my froward eye
With sweet and scarless sky;
Stir in my ears, speak there
Of God's love, O live air,
Of patience, penance, prayer:
World-mothering air, air wild,
Wound with thee, in thee isled,
Fold home, fast fold thy child.

38.[89]
To what serves Mortal Beauty?

To what serves mortal beauty— | dangerous; does set danc-
ing blood—the O-seal-that-so | feature, flung prouder form
Than Purcell tune lets tread to? | See: it does this: keeps warm
Men's wits to the things that are; | what good means—where a glance
Master more may than gaze, | gaze out of countenance.
Those lovely lads once, wet-fresh | windfalls of war's storm,
How then should Gregory, a father, | have gleanèd else from swarm-
ed Rome? But God to a nation | dealt that day's dear chance.
    To man, that needs would worship | block or barren stone,
Our law says: Love what are | love's worthiest, were all known;

[89] "(Common rhythm highly stressed: sonnet.) Aug. 23, '85." Autograph in
A.—Another autograph in B with a few variants from which A was chosen, the
deletion of alternatives incomplete. Thirdly a copy sent to R. W. D., apparently
later than A, but with errors of copy. The text given is guided by this version
in D, and *needs* in line 9 is substituted there for the *once* in A and B, probably
because of *once* in line 6.—Original draft exists in H, on same page with 39 and
40. [Note by R. Bridges.]

World's loveliest—men's selves. Self | flashes off frame and face.
What do then? how meet beauty? | Merely meet it; own,
Home at heart, heaven's sweet gift; | then leave, let that alone.
Yea, wish that though, wish all, | God's better beauty, grace.

39.[90]
(The Soldier)

Yes. Why` do we áll, seeing of a soldier, bless him? bless
Our redcoats, our tars? Both these being, the greater part,
But frail clay, nay but foul clay. Here it is: the heart,
Since, proud, it calls the calling manly, gives a guess
That, hopes that, makesbelieve, the men must be no less;
It fancies, feigns, deems, dears the artist after his art;
And fain will find as sterling all as all is smart,
And scarlet wear the spirit of wár thére express.

Mark Christ our King. He knows war, served this
   soldiering through;
He of all can handle a rope best. There he bides in bliss
Now, and séeing somewhére some mán do all that man can do,
For love he leans forth, needs his neck must fall on, kiss,
And cry "O Christ-done deed! So God-made-flesh does too:
Were I come o'er again" cries Christ "it should be this."

---

[90] "Clongower, Aug. 1885." Autograph in H, with a few corrections which I have
taken for lines 6 and 7, of which the first draft runs:
   It fancies; it deems; dears the artist after his art;
   So feigns it finds as, &c.
The MS. marks the caesural place in ten of the lines: in line 2, between *Both* and
these. l. 3, at the full stop. l. 6, *fancies, feigns, deems,* take three stresses. l. 11, after
man. In line 7 I have added a comma at *smart*. In l. 10 I have substituted *handle*
for *reave* of MS.; and in l. 13, have hyphened *God made flesh*. No title in MS.
[Note by R. Bridges.]

40.[91]
(Carrion Comfort)

Not, I'll not, carrion comfort, Despair, not feast on thee;
Not untwist—slack they may be—these last strands of man
In me ór, most weary, cry *I can no more.* I can;
Can something, hope, wish day come, not choose not to be.
But ah, but O thou terrible, why wouldst thou rude on me
Thy wring-world right foot rock? lay a lionlimb against me? scan
With darksome devouring eyes my bruisèd bones? and fan,
O in turns of tempest, me heaped there;
   me frantic to avoid thee and flee?

Why? That my chaff might fly; my grain lie, sheer and clear.
Nay in all that toil, that coil, since (seems) I kissed the rod,
Hand rather, my heart lo! lapped strength, stole joy,
   would laugh, chéer.
Cheer whom though? the hero whose heaven-handling
   flung me, fóot tród
Me? or me that fought him? O which one? is it each one?
   That night, that year
Of now done darkness I wretch lay wrestling with (my God!)
   my God.

41.[92]
"No worst, there is none"

No worst, there is none. Pitched past pitch of grief,
More pangs will, schooled at forepangs, wilder wring.
Comforter, where, where is your comforting?
Mary, mother of us, where is your relief?

---

[91] Autograph in H, in three versions. 1st, deleted draft. 2nd, a complete version, both on same page with 38 and 39. 3rd, with 41 on another sheet, final (?) revision carried only to end of l. 12 (two detached lines on reverse). Text is this last with last two lines from the 2nd version. Date must be 1885, and this is probably the sonnet "written in blood," of which he wrote in May of that year.—I have added the title and the hyphen in *heaven-handling.* [Note by R. Bridges.]

[92] Autograph in H, on same page as third draft of 40. One undated draft with corrections embodied in the text here.—l. 5, at end are some marks which look like a hyphen and a comma: no title. [Note by R. Bridges.]

My cries heave, herds-long; huddle in a main, a chief
Woe, world-sorrow; on an age-old anvil wince and sing—
Then lull, then leave off. Fury had shrieked "No ling-
ering! Let me be fell: force I must be brief."

O the mind, mind has mountains; cliffs of fall
Frightful, sheer, no-man-fathomed. Hold them cheap
May who ne'er hung there. Nor does long our small
Durance deal with that steep or deep. Here! creep,
Wretch, under a comfort serves in a whirlwind: all
Life death does end and each day dies with sleep.

42.[93]
Tom's Garland;
upon the Unemployed

Tom—garlanded with squat and surly steel
Tom; then Tom's fallowbootfellow piles pick

---

[93] "Sonnet: common rhythm, but with hurried feet: two codas. Dromore, Sept.
'87." With full title, A.—Another autograph in B is identical. In line 9 there is a
strong accent on *I.*—l. 10, the capital initial of *country* is doubtful.—Rhythmical
marks omitted. The author's own explanation of this poem may be read in a letter
written to me from "Dublin, Feb. 10, '88:...I laughed outright and often, but very
sardonically, to think you and the Canon [R. W. Dixon] could not construe my
last sonnet; that he had to write to you for a crib. It is plain I must go no further
on this road: if you and he cannot understand me who will? Yet, declaimed, the
strange constructions would be dramatic and effective. Must I interpret it? It
means then that, as St. Paul and Plato and Hobbes and everybody says, the commonwealth or well-ordered human society is like one man; a body with many
members and each its function; some higher, some lower, but all honourable, from
the honour which belongs to the whole. The head is the sovereign, who has no
superior but God and from heaven receives his or her authority: we must then
imagine this head as bare (see St. Paul much on this) and covered, so to say, only
with the sun and stars, of which the crown is a symbol, which is an ornament
but not a covering; it has an enormous hat or skullcap, the vault of heaven. The
foot is the day-labourer, and this is armed with hobnail boots, because it has to
wear and be worn by the ground; which again is symbolical; for it is navvies or
day-labourers who, on the great scale or in gangs and millions, mainly trench,
tunnel, blast, and in other ways disfigure, 'mammock' the earth and, on a small
scale, singly, and superficially stamp it with their footprints. And the 'garlands'
of nails they wear are therefore the visible badge of the place they fill, the lowest
in the commonwealth. But this place still shares the common honour, and if it
wants one advantage, glory or public fame, makes up for it by another, ease of
mind, absence of care; and these things are symbolised by the gold and the iron
garlands. (O, once explained, how clear it all is!) Therefore the scene of the poem
is laid at evening, when they are giving over work and one after another pile their
picks, with which they earn their living, and swing off home, knocking sparks
out of mother earth not now by labour and of choice but by the mere footing,
being strongshod and making no hardship of hardness, taking all easy. And so to
supper and bed. Here comes a violent but effective hyperbaton or suspension, in
which the action of the mind mimics that of the labourer—surveys his lot, low
but free from care; then by a sudden strong act throws it over the shoulder or
tosses it away as a light matter. The witnessing of which lightheartedness makes
me indignant with the fools of Radical Levellers. But presently I remember that
this is all very well for those who are in, however low in, the Commonwealth
and share in any way the common weal; but that the curse of our times is that
many do not share it, that they are outcasts from it and have neither security nor
splendour; that they share care with the high and obscurity with the low, but
wealth or comfort with neither. And this state of things, I say, is the origin of
Loafers, Tramps, Cornerboys, Roughs, Socialists and other pests of society. And
I think that it is a very pregnant sonnet, and in point of execution very highly
wrought, too much so, I am afraid....G. M. H." [Note by R. Bridges.]

By him and rips out rockfire homeforth—sturdy Dick;
Tom Heart-at-ease, Tom Navvy: he is all for his meal
Sure, 's bed now. Low be it: lustily he his low lot (feel
That ne'er need hunger, Tom; Tom seldom sick,
Seldomer heartsore; that treads through, prickproof, thick
Thousands of thorns, thoughts) swings though. Commonweal
Little I reck ho! lacklevel in, if all had bread:
What! Country is honour enough in all us—lordly head,
With heaven's lights high hung round, or, mother-ground
That mammocks, mighty foot. But no way sped,
Nor mind nor mainstrength; gold go garlanded
With, perilous, O nó; nor yet plod safe shod sound;
    Undenizened, beyond bound
Of earth's glory, earth's ease, all; no one, nowhere,
In wide the world's weal; rare gold, bold steel, bare
    In both; care, but share care—
This, by Despair, bred Hangdog dull; by Rage,
Manwolf, worse; and their packs infest the age.

43.[94]
Harry Ploughman

Hard as hurdle arms, with a broth of goldish flue
Breathed round; the rack of ribs; the scooped flank; lank
Rope-over thigh; knee-nave; and barrelled shank—
    Head and foot, shoulder and shank—
By a grey eye's heed steered well, one crew, fall to;
Stand at stress. Each limb's barrowy brawn, his thew
That onewhere curded, onewhere sucked or sank—
    Soared or sank—,
Though as a beechbole firm, finds his, as at a roll-call, rank
And features, in flesh, what deed he each must do—
    His sinew-service where do.

He leans to it, Harry bends, look. Back, elbow, and liquid waist
In him, all quail to the wallowing o' the plough:
    's cheek crimsons; curls
Wag or crossbridle, in a wind lifted, windlaced—
    See his wind- lilylocks -laced;

---

[94] "Dromore, Sept. 1887." Autograph in A.—Autograph in B has several emendations written over without deletion of original. Text is B with these corrections, which are all good.—line 10, *features* is the verb.—13, *'s* is *his.* I have put a colon at *plough,* in place of author's full stop, for the convenience of reader.—15=*his lilylocks windlaced.* "Saxo cere- comminuit -brum."—17, *Them. These,* A.—In the last three lines the grammar intends, "How his churl's grace governs the movement of his booted (in bluff hide) feet, as they are matched in a race with the wet shining furrow overturned by the share." G. M. H. thought well of this sonnet and wrote on Sept. 28, 1887: "I have been touching up some old sonnets you have never seen and have within a few days done the whole of one, I hope, very good one and most of another; the one finished is a direct picture of a ploughman, without afterthought. But when you read it let me know if there is anything like it in Walt Whitman; as perhaps there may be, and I should be sorry for that." And again on Oct. 11, '87: "I will enclose the sonnet on Harry Ploughman, in which burden-lines (they might be recited by a chorus) are freely used: there is in this very heavily loaded sprung rhythm a call for their employment. The rhythm of this sonnet, which is altogether for recital, and not for perusal (as by nature verse should be), is very highly studied. From much considering it I can no longer gather any impression of it: perhaps it will strike you as intolerably violent and artificial." And again on Nov. 6, '87: "I want Harry Ploughman to be a vivid figure before the mind's eye; if he is not that the sonnet fails. The difficulties are of syntax no doubt. Dividing a compound word by a clause sandwiched into it was a desperate deed, I feel, and I do not feel that it was an unquestionable success." [Note by R. Bridges.]

Churlsgrace, too, child of Amansstrength, how it hangs or hurls
Them—broad in bluff hide his frowning feet lashed! raced
With, along them, cragiron under and cold furls—
    With-a-fountain's shining-shot furls.

44.[95]
"To seem the stranger lies my lot..."

To seem the stranger lies my lot, my life
Among strangers. Father and mother dear,
Brothers and sisters are in Christ not near
And he my peace my parting, sword and strife.
    England, whose honour O all my heart woos, wife
To my creating thought, would neither hear
Me, were I pleading, plead nor do I: I wear-
y of idle a being but by where wars are rife.

    I am in Ireland now; now I am at a third
Remove. Not but in all removes I can
Kind love both give and get. Only what word
Wisest my heart breeds dark heaven's baffling ban
Bars or hell's spell thwarts. This to hoard unheard,
Heard unheeded, leaves me a lonely began.

45.[96]
"I wake and feel the fell of dark..."

I wake and feel the fell of dark, not day.
What hours, O what black hours we have spent
This night! what sights you, heart, saw; ways you went!
And more must, in yet longer light's delay.

---

[95] These four sonnets ([Nos. 44, 45, 46, 47] together with No. 56) are all written
undated in a small hand on the two sides of a half-sheet of common sermon-paper,
in the order in which they are here printed. They probably date back as early as
1885, and may be all, or some of them, those referred to in a letter of Sept. 1,
1885: "I shall shortly have some sonnets to send you, five or more. Four of these
came like inspirations unbidden and against my will. And in the life I lead now,
which is one of a continually jaded and harassed mind, if in any leisure I try to
do anything I make no way—nor with my work, alas! but so it must be." I have
no certain nor single identification of date. [Note by R. Bridges.]

[96] See note to No. 44.

With witness I speak this. But where I say
Hours I mean years, mean life. And my lament
Is cries countless, cries like dead letters sent
To dearest him that lives alas! away.

I am gall, I am heartburn. God's most deep decree
Bitter would have me taste: my taste was me;
Bones built in me, flesh filled, blood brimmed the curse.
    Selfyeast of spirit a dull dough sours. I see
The lost are like this, and their scourge to be
As I am mine, their sweating selves; but worse.

46.[97]
"Patience, hard thing!..."

Patience, hard thing! the hard thing but to pray,
But bid for, Patience is! Patience who asks
Wants war, wants wounds; weary his times, his tasks;
To do without, take tosses, and obey.
    Rare patience roots in these, and, these away,
Nowhere. Natural heart's ivy, Patience masks
Our ruins of wrecked past purpose. There she basks
Purple eyes and seas of liquid leaves all day.

We hear our hearts grate on themselves: it kills
To bruise them dearer. Yet the rebellious wills
Of us we do bid God bend to him even so.
    And where is he who more and more distils
Delicious kindness?—He is patient. Patience fills
His crisp combs, and that comes those ways we know.

---

[97] *Patience is.* The initial capital is mine, and the comma after ivy in line 6. No title.
[Note by R. Bridges.] (See also Bridges's note to No. 44.)

47.[98]
"My own heart let me have more pity on..."

My own heart let me have more pity on; let
Me live to my sad self hereafter kind,
Charitable; not live this tormented mind
With this tormented mind tormenting yet.
   I cast for comfort I can no more get
By groping round my comfortless, than blind
Eyes in their dark can day or thirst can find
Thirst's all-in-all in all a world of wet.

Soul, self; come, poor Jackself, I do advise
You, jaded, let be; call off thoughts awhile
Elsewhere; leave comfort root-room; let joy size
At God knows when to God knows what; whose smile
's not wrung, see you; unforeseen times rather—as skies
Betweenpie mountains—lights a lovely mile.

---

[98] I have added the comma after *comfortless;* that word has the same grammatical value as *dark* in the following line. "I cast for comfort, (which) I can no more find in my comfortless (world) than a blind man in his dark world...."—l. 10, MS. accents *let.*—13 and 14, the text here from a good correction separately written (as far as *mountains*) on the top margin of No. 56. There are therefore two writings of *betweenpie,* a strange word, in which *pie* apparently makes a compound verb with *between,* meaning "as the sky seen between dark mountains is brightly dappled," the grammar such as *intervariegates* would make. This word might have delighted William Barnes, if the verb "to pie" existed. It seems not to exist, and to be forbidden by homophonic absurdities. [Note by R. Bridges.] (See note to No. 44.)

48.[99]
That Nature is a Heraclitean Fire and of the comfort of the Resurrection

Cloud-puffball, torn tufts, tossed pillows |
   flaunt forth, then chevy on an air-
built thoroughfare: heaven-roysterers, in gay-gangs |
   they throng; they glitter in marches.
Down roughcast, down dazzling whitewash, |
   wherever an elm arches,
Shivelights and shadowtackle in long | lashes lace, lance, and pair.
Delightfully the bright wind boisterous |
   ropes, wrestles, beats earth bare
Of yestertempest's creases; in pool and rut peel parches
Squandering ooze to squeezed |
   dough, crust, dust; stanches, starches
Squadroned masks and manmarks | treadmire toil there
Footfretted in it. Million-fuelèd, | nature's bonfire burns on.
But quench her bonniest, dearest | to her, her clearest-selvèd spark
Man, how fast his firedint, | his mark on mind, is gone!
Both are in an unfathomable, all is in an enormous dark
Drowned. O pity and indig | nation! Manshape, that shone
Sheer off, disseveral, a star, | death blots black out; nor mark
   Is any of him at all so stark
But vastness blurs and time | beats level.
   Enough! the Resurrection,
A heart's-clarion! Away grief's gasping, | joyless days, dejection.

---

[99] "(Sprung rhythm, with many outrides and hurried feet: sonnet with two *[sic]* codas.) July 26, 1888. Co. Dublin. The last sonnet [this] provisional only." Autograph in A.—I have found no other copy nor trace of draft. The title is from A.—line 6, construction obscure. *rutpeel* may be a compound word, MS. uncertain.—8, ? omitted relative pronoun. If so="the manmarks that treadmire toil foot-fretted in it." MS. does not hyphen nor quite join up *foot* with *fretted*.—12. MS. has no caesural mark.—On Aug. 18, '88, he wrote: "I will now go to bed, the more so as I am going to preach tomorrow and put plainly to a Highland congregation of MacDonalds, Mackintoshes, Mackillops, and the rest what I am putting not at all so plainly to the rest of the world, or rather to you and Canon Dixon, in a sonnet in sprung rhythm with two codas." And again on Sept. 25, '88: "Lately I sent you a sonnet on the Heraclitean Fire, in which a great deal of early Greek philosophical thought was distilled; but the liquor of the distillation did not taste very Greek, did it? The effect of studying masterpieces is to make me admire and do otherwise. So it must be on every original artist to some degree, on me to a marked degree. Perhaps then more reading would only *refine my singularity,* which is not what you want." Note, that the sonnet has three codas, not two. [Note by R. Bridges.]

Across my foundering deck shone
A beacon, an eternal beam. | Flesh fade, and mortal trash
Fall to the residuary worm; | world's wildfire, leave but ash:
  In a flash, at a trumpet crash,
I am all at once what Christ is, | since he was what I am, and
This Jack, joke, poor potsherd, | patch, matchwood, immortal diamond,
  Is immortal diamond.

49.[100]

In honour of
St. Alphonsus Rodriguez
Laybrother of the Society of Jesus

Honour is flashed off exploit, so we say;
And those strokes once that gashed flesh or galled shield
Should tongue that time now, trumpet now that field,
And, on the fighter, forge his glorious day.
On Christ they do and on the martyr may;
But be the war within, the brand we wield
Unseen, the heroic breast not outward-steeled,
Earth hears no hurtle then from fiercest fray.

  Yet God (that hews mountain and continent,
Earth, all, out; who, with trickling increment,
Veins violets and tall trees makes more and more)
Could crowd career with conquest while there went
Those years and years by of world without event
That in Majorca Alfonso watched the door.

---

[100]Text from autograph with title and "upon the first falling of his feast after his canonization" in B. An autograph in A, sent Oct. 3 from Dublin asking for immediate criticism, because the sonnet had to go to Majorca. "I ask your opinion of a sonnet written to order on the occasion of the first feast since his canonisation proper of St. Alphonsus Rodriguez, a laybrother of our Order, who for 40 years acted as hall porter to the College of Palma in Majorca; he was, it is believed, much favoured by God with heavenly light and much persecuted by evil spirits. The sonnet (I say it snorting) aims at being intelligible." And on Oct. 9, '88, "I am obliged for your criticisms, 'contents of which noted,' indeed acted on. I have improved the sestet....(He defends 'hew')...at any rate whatever is markedly featured in stone or what is like stone is most naturally said to be hewn, and to *shape,* itself, means in old English to hew and the Hebrew *bara* to create, even, properly means to hew. But life and living things are not naturally said to be hewn: they grow, and their growth is by trickling increment....The (first) line now stands 'Glory is a flame off exploit, so we say.'" [Note by R. Bridges.]

50.[101]
"Thou art indeed just, Lord..."

*Justus quidem tu es, Domine, si disputem tecum: verumtamen justa loquar
ad te: Quare via impiorum prosperatur? &c.*

Thou art indeed just, Lord, if I contend
With thee; but, sir, so what I plead is just.
Why do sinners' ways prosper? and why must
Disappointment all I endeavour end?
   Wert thou my enemy, O thou my friend,
How wouldst thou worse, I wonder, than thou dost
Defeat, thwart me? Oh, the sots and thralls of lust
Do in spare hours more thrive than I that spend,
Sir, life upon thy cause. See, banks and brakes
Now, leavèd how thick! lacèd they are again
With fretty chervil, look, and fresh wind shakes
Them; birds build—but not I build; no, but strain,
Time's eunuch, and not breed one work that wakes.
Mine, O thou lord of life, send my roots rain.

51.[102]
To R. B.

The fine delight that fathers thought; the strong
Spur, live and lancing like the blowpipe flame,
Breathes once and, quenchèd faster than it came,
Leaves yet the mind a mother of immortal song.
Nine months she then, nay years, nine years she long
Within her wears, bears, cares and moulds the same:
The widow of an insight lost she lives, with aim
Now known and hand at work now never wrong.
   Sweet fire the sire of muse, my soul needs this;
I want the one rapture of an inspiration.

---

[101]The poem has been dated March 17, 1889. The Latin epigraph is from the first
verse of Jeremiah 12; Hopkins translates it in the first two and a half lines.
[BB.]

[102]"To R. B. April 22, '89." Autograph in A. This, the last poem sent to me, came
on April 29.— No other copy, but the working drafts in H.—In line 6 the word
moulds was substituted by me for *combs* of original, when the sonnet was published
by Miles [in *The Poets and Poetry of the Century*]; and I leave it, having no doubt
that G. M. H. would have made some such alteration. [Note by R. Bridges.]

O then if in my lagging lines you miss
The roll, the rise, the carol, the creation,
My winter world, that scarcely breathes that bliss
Now, yields you, with some sighs, our explanation.

~

Unfinished Poems & Fragments

~

52.[103]
Summa

The best ideal is the true
And other truth is none.
All glory be ascribèd to
The holy Three in One.

53.
"What being in rank-old nature should earlier have that breath been"

What being in rank-old nature should earlier have that breath been
That hére pérsonal tells off these heart-song powerful peals?—
A bush-browed, beetle-brówed bíllow is it?
With a soúth-wésterly wínd blústering, with a tide rolls reels
Of crumbling, fore-foundering, thundering all-surfy seas in; seen
Únderneath, their glassy barrel, of a fairy green.

Or a jaunting vaunting vaulting assaulting trumpet telling.

---

[103]This poem had, I believe, the ambitious design which its title suggests. What
was done of it was destroyed, with other things, when he joined the Jesuits.
My copy is a contemporary autograph of 16 lines, written when he was still an
undergraduate; I give the first four. A. [Note by R. Bridges.]

54.[104]

On the Portrait of Two Beautiful Young People

a Brother and Sister

O I admire and sorrow! The heart's eye grieves
Discovering you, dark tramplers, tyrant years.
A juice rides rich through bluebells, in vine leaves,
And beauty's dearest veriest vein is tears.

Happy the father, mother of these! Too fast:
Not that, but thus far, all with frailty, blest
In one fair fall; but, for time's aftercast,
Creatures all heft, hope, hazard, interest.

And are they thus? The fine, the fingering beams
Their young delightful hour do feature down
That fleeted else like day-dissolvèd dreams
Or ringlet-race on burling Barrow brown.

She leans on him with such contentment fond
As well the sister sits, would well the wife;
His looks, the soul's own letters, see beyond,
Gaze on, and fall directly forth on life.

But ah, bright forelock, cluster that you are
Of favoured make and mind and health and youth,
Where lies your landmark, seamark, or soul's star?
There's none but truth can stead you. Christ is truth.

There's none but good can bé good, both for you
And what sways with you, maybe this sweet maid;
None good but God—a warning wavèd to
One once that was found wanting when Good weighed.

Man lives that list, that leaning in the will
No wisdom can forecast by gauge or guess,
The selfless self of self, most strange, most still,
Fast furled and all foredrawn to No or Yes.

Your feast of; that most in you earnest eye
May but call on your banes to more carouse.
Worst will the best. What worm was here, we cry,
To have havoc-pocked so, see, the hung-heavenward boughs?

---

[104]"On the Portrait &c. Monastereven, Co. Kildare, Christmas, '86." Autograph
with full title, no corrections, in A. Early drafts in H. [Note by R. Bridges.]

Enough: corruption was the world's first woe.
What need I strain my heart beyond my ken?
O but I bear my burning witness though
Against the wild and wanton work of men.

55.[105]

"The sea took pity: it interposed with doom"

The sea took pity: it interposed with doom:
"I have tall daughters dear that heed my hand:
Let Winter wed one, sow them in her womb,
And she shall child them on the New-world strand."

56.[106]
(Ash-boughs)

a.

Not of all my eyes see, wándering on the world,
Is anything a milk to the mind so, só sighs déep
Poetry to it, as a tree whose boughs break in the sky.
Say it is ashboughs: whether on a December day and furled
Fast ór they in clammyish lashtender combs creep
Apart wide and new-nestle at heaven most high.
They touch heaven, tabour on it; how their talons sweep
The smouldering enormous winter welkin! May
Mells blue and snowwhite through them, a fringe and fray
Of greenery: it is old earth's groping towards the steep
   Heaven whom she childs us by.

---

[105]Undated pencil scrap in H. [Note by R. Bridges.]

[106](My title). In H in two versions; first as a curtal sonnet (like 13 and 22) on same sheet with the four sonnets 44–47, and preceding them: second, an apparently later version in the same metre on a page by itself; with expanded variation from seventh line, making thirteen lines for eleven. I print the whole of this second MS., and have put brackets to show what I think would make the best version of the poem: for if the bracketed words were omitted the original curtal sonnet form would be preserved and carry the good corrections.—The uncomfortable eye in the added portion was perhaps to be worked as a vocative referring to first line (?). [Note by R. Bridges.] (See also Bridges's note to No. 44.)

b. (Variant from line 7.)

They touch, they tabour on it, hover on it[; here, there hurled],
   With talons sweep
The smouldering enormous winter welkin. [Eye,
   But more cheer is when] May
Mells blue with snowwhite through their fringe and fray
Of greenery and old earth gropes for, grasps at steep
   Heaven with it whom she childs things by.

57.[107]
"Hope holds to Christ the mind's own mirror out"

Hope holds to Christ the mind's own mirror out
To take His lovely likeness more and more.
It will not well, so she would bring about
An ever brighter burnish than before
And turns to wash it from her welling eyes
And breathes the blots off all with sighs on sighs.

Her glass is blest but she as good as blind
Holds till hand aches and wonders what is there;
Her glass drinks light, she darkles down behind,
All of her glorious gainings unaware.
I told you that she turned her mirror dim
Betweenwhiles, but she sees herself not Him.

---

[107] In H, a torn undated scrap which carries a vivid splotch of local colour.—line 4, a variant has *A growing burnish brighter than.* [Note by R. Bridges.]

58.[108]
St. Winefred's Well

Act I. Sc. I

Enter Teryth from riding, Winefred following.

TERYTH. What is it, Gwen, my girl? why do you hover and
  haunt me?

WINEFRED. You came by Caerwys, sir?

TERYTH.   I came by Caerwys.

WINEFRED.   There
  Some messenger there might have met you from my uncle.

TERYTH. Your uncle met the messenger—met me;
  and this the message:
    Lord Beuno comes to-night.

WINEFRED.   To-night, sir!

TERYTH. Soon, now: therefore
  Have all things ready in his room.

WINEFRED.   There needs but little doing.

TERYTH. Let what there needs be done. Stay! with him
  one companion,
  His deacon, Dirvan Warm: twice over must the welcome be,
    But both will share one cell.—This was good news, Gwenvrewi.

WINEFRED. Ah yes!

TERYTH.   Why, get thee gone then; tell thy mother I want her.

Exit WINEFRED.

---

[108]G. M. H. began a tragedy on St. Winefred Oct. '79, for which he subsequently
  wrote the chorus, No. 36, above. He was at it again in 1881, and had mentioned
  the play in his letters, and when, some years later, I determined to write my *Feast
  of Bacchus* in six-stressed verse, I sent him a sample of it, and asked him to let me
  see what he had made of the measure. The MS. which he sent me, April 1, 1885,
  was copied, and that copy is the text in this book, from A, the original not being
  discoverable. It may therefore contain copyist's errors. Twenty years later, when I
  was writing my *Demeter* for the lady-students at Somerville College, I remembered
  the first line of Caradoc's soliloquy, and made some use of it. On the other hand
  the broken line *I have read her eyes* in my 1st part of *Nero* is proved by date to be
  a coincidence, and not a reminiscence.—Caradoc was to "die impenitent, struck
  by the finger of God." [Note by R. Bridges.]

No man has such a daughter. The fathers of the world
Call no such maiden "mine." The deeper grows her dearness
And more and more times laces round and round my heart,
The more some monstrous hand gropes with clammy
    fingers there,
Tampering with those sweet bines, draws them out, strains them,
    strains them;
Meantime some tongue cries "What, Teryth! what, thou poor
    fond father!
How when this bloom, this honeysuckle, that rides the air so
    rich about thee,
Is all, all sheared away, thus!" Then I sweat for fear.
Or else a funeral, and yet 'tis not a funeral,
Some pageant which takes tears and I must foot with feeling that
Alive or dead my girl is carried in it, endlessly
Goes marching thro' my mind. What sense is this? It has none.
This is too much the father; nay the mother. Fanciful!
I here forbid my thoughts to fool themselves with fears.

Enter Gwenlo.

. . . .

Act II.

*Scene, a wood ending in a steep bank over a dry dean. Winefred having
been murdered within, re-enter Caradoc with a bloody sword.*

Caradoc. My heart, where have we been? What have we seen,
    my mind?
  What stroke has Caradoc's right arm dealt? what done?
    Head of a rebel
  Struck off it has; written upon lovely limbs,
  In bloody letters, lessons of earnest, of revenge;
  Monuments of my earnest, records of my revenge,
  On one that went against me whéreas I had warned her—
  Warned her! well she knew. I warned her of this work.
  What work? what harm's done? There is no harm done, none yet;
  Perhaps we struck no blow, Gwenvrewi lives perhaps;
  To makebelieve my mood was—mock. O I might think so
  But here, here is a workman from his day's task sweats.
  Wiped I am sure this was; it seems not well; for still,
  Still the scarlet swings and dances on the blade.
  So be it. Thou steel, thou butcher,
  I cán scour thee, fresh burnish thee, sheathe thee in thy dark lair;
    these drops

Never, never, never in their blue banks again.
The woeful, Cradock, O the woeful word! Then what,
What have we seen? Her head, sheared from her shoulders, fall,
And lapped in shining hair, roll to the bank's edge; then
Down the beetling banks, like water in waterfalls,
It stooped and flashed and fell and ran like water away.
Her eyes, oh and her eyes!
In all her beauty, and sunlight to it is a pit, den, darkness,
Foam-falling is not fresh to it, rainbow by it not beaming,
In all her body, I say, no place was like her eyes,
No piece matched those eyes kept most part much cast down
But, being lifted, immortal, of immortal brightness.
Several times I saw them, thrice or four times turning;
Round and round they came and flashed towards heaven:
    O there,
There they did appeal. Therefore airy vengeances
Are afoot; heaven-vault fast purpling portends, and what
    first lightning
Any instant falls means me. And I do not repent;
I do not and I will not repent, not repent.
The blame bear who aroused me. What I have done violent
I have like a lion done, lionlike done,
Honouring an uncontrolled royal wrathful nature,
Mantling passion in a grandeur, crimson grandeur.
Now be my pride then perfect, all one piece. Henceforth
In a wide world of defiance Caradoc lives alone,
Loyal to his own soul, laying his own law down, no law nor
Lord now curb him for ever. O daring! O deep insight!
What is virtue? Valour; only the heart valiant.
And right? Only resolution; will, his will unwavering
Who, like me, knowing his nature to the heart home,
    nature's business,
Despatches with no flinching. But will flesh, O can flesh
Second this fiery strain? Not always; O no no!
We cannot live this life out; sometimes we must weary
And in this darksome world what comfort can I find?
Down this darksome world cómfort whére can I find
When 'ts light I quenched; its rose, time's one rich rose,
    my hand,
By her bloom, fast by her fresh, her fleecèd bloom,
Hideous dashed down, leaving earth a winter withering
With no now, no Gwenvrewi. I must miss her most
That might have spared her were it but for passion-sake. Yes,

To hunger and not have, yét hope ón for, to storm and
   strive and
Be at every assault fresh foiled, worse flung, deeper disappointed,
The turmoil and the torment, it has, I swear, a sweetness,
Keeps a kind of joy in it, a zest, an edge, an ecstasy,
Next after sweet success. I am not left even this;
I all my being have hacked in half with her neck: one part,
Reason, selfdisposal, choice of better or worse way,
Is corpse now, cannot change; my other self, this soul,
Life's quick, this kínd, this kéen self-feeling,
With dreadful distillation of thoughts sour as blood,
Must all day long taste murder. What do nów then? Do? Nay,
Deed-bound I am; one deed treads all down here cramps
   all doing. What do? Not yield,
Not hope, not pray; despair; ay, that: brazen despair out,
Brave all, and take what comes—as here this rabble is come,
Whose bloods I reck no more of, no more rank with hers
Than sewers with sacred oils. Mankind, that mobs,
   comes. Come!

Enter A CROWD, AMONG THEM TERYTH, GWENLO, BEUNO.

. . . .

*AFTER WINEFRED'S RAISING FROM THE DEAD AND THE BREAKING
OUT OF THE FOUNTAIN.*

BEUNO. O now while skies are blue, now while seas are salt,
While rushy rains shall fall or brooks shall fleet from fountains,
While sick men shall cast sighs, of sweet health all despairing,
While blind men's eyes shall thirst after daylight, draughts
   of daylight,
Or deaf ears shall desire that lipmusic that 's lost upon them,
While cripples are, while lepers, dancers in dismal limb-dance,
Fallers in dreadful frothpits, waterfearers wild,
Stone, palsy, cancer, cough, lung wasting, womb not bearing,
Rupture, running sores, what more? in brief; in burden,
As long as men are mortal and God merciful,
So long to this sweet spot, this leafy lean-over,
This Dry Dene, now no longer dry nor dumb, but moist
   and musical
With the uproll and the downcarol of day and night delivering
Water, which keeps thy name, (for not in róck wrítten,
But in pale water, frail water, wild rash and reeling water,
That will not wear a print, that will not stain a pen,

Thy venerable record, virgin, is recorded).
Here to this holy well shall pilgrimages be,
And not from purple Wales only nor from elmy England,
But from beyond seas, Erin, France and Flanders, everywhere,
Pilgrims, still pilgrims, móre pílgrims, still more poor pilgrims.

. . . .

What sights shall be when some that swung, wretches, on crutches
Their crutches shall cast from them, on heels of air departing,
Or they go rich as roseleaves hence that loathsome cáme hither!
Not now to náme even
Those dearer, more divine boons whose haven the heart is.

. . . .

As sure as what is most sure, sure as that spring primroses
Shall new-dapple next year, sure as to-morrow morning,
Amongst come-back-again things, thíngs with a revival, things
with a recovery,
Thy name…

. . . .

59.[109]

"What shall I do for the land that bred me"

What shall I do for the land that bred me,
Her homes and fields that folded and fed me?—
Be under her banner and live for her honour:
Under her banner I'll live for her honour.
   Chorus. Under her banner live for her honour.

Not the pleasure, the pay, the plunder,
But country and flag, the flag I am under—
There is the shilling that finds me willing
To follow a banner and fight for honour.
   Chorus. We follow her banner, we fight for her honour.

---

[109]Sent me in a letter with his own melody and a note on the poem. "This is not final of course. Perhaps the name of England is too exclusive." Date Clongower, Aug. 1885. A. [Note by R. Bridges.]

Call me England's fame's fond lover,
Her fame to keep, her fame to recover.
Spend me or end me what God shall send me,
But under her banner I live for her honour.
    CHORUS. Under her banner we march for her honour.

Where is the field I must play the man on?
O welcome there their steel or cannon.
Immortal beauty is death with duty,
If under her banner I fall for her honour.
    CHORUS. Under her banner we fall for her honour.

60.[110]
"The times are nightfall, look, their light grows less"

The times are nightfall, look, their light grows less;
The times are winter, watch, a world undone:
They waste, they wither worse; they as they run
Or bring more or more blazon man's distress.
And I not help. Nor word now of success:
All is from wreck, here, there, to rescue one—
Work which to see scarce so much as begun
Makes welcome death, does dear forgetfulness.
Or what is else? There is your world within.
There rid the dragons, root out there the sin.
Your will is law in that small commonweal...

[110]Revised and corrected draft in H. The first two lines are corrected from the
original opening in old syllabic verse:
    The times are nightfall and the light grows less;
    The times are winter and a world undone;
[Note by R. Bridges.]

61.[111]
Cheery Beggar

Beyond Mágdalen and by the Bridge, on a place called there the Plain,
  In Summer, in a burst of summertime
  Following falls and falls of rain,
When the air was sweet-and-sour of the flown fineflower of
Those goldnails and their gaylinks that hang along a lime;

      . . . .

  The motion of that man's heart is fine
  Whom want could not make píne, píne
That struggling should not sear him, a gift should cheer him
Like that poor pocket of pence, poor pence of mine.

        . . . .

62.[112]
"Denis, whose motionable, alert, most vaulting wit"

Denis, whose motionable, alert, most vaulting wit
Caps occasion with an intellectual fit.
Yet Arthur is a Bowman: his three-heeled timber'll hit
The bald and bóld blínking gold when áll's dóne
Right rooting in the bare butt's wincing navel in the sight of the sun.

       . . . .

---

[111]Undated draft with much correction, in H. Text is the outcome.
  [Note by R. Bridges.]

[112]No. 62 ("Denis, whose motionable, alert, most vaulting wit") and No. 63 ("The
  furl of fresh-leaved dogrose down"): These are my interpretation of the intention
  of some unfinished disordered verses on a sheet of paper in H. In 63, line 1, *furl*
  is I think unmistakable: an apparently rejected earlier version had *Soft childhood's
  carmine, dew-drift down.* [Note by R. Bridges.]

63.[113]
"The furl of fresh-leaved dogrose down"

The furl of fresh-leavéd dogrose down
His cheeks the forth-and-flaunting sun
Had swarthed about with lion-brown
   Before the Spring was done.

His locks like all a ravel-rope's-end,
   With hempen strands in spray—
Fallow, foam-fallow, hanks—fall'n off their ranks,
   Swung down at a disarray.

Or like a juicy and jostling shock
   Of bluebells sheaved in May
Or wind-long fleeces on the flock
   A day off shearing day.

Then over his turnèd temples—here—
   Was a rose, or, failing that,
Rough-Robin or five-lipped campion clear
   For a beauty-bow to his hat,
And the sunlight sidled, like dewdrops, like dandled diamonds
   Through the sieve of the straw of the plait.

      . . . .

64.[114]
The Woodlark

Teevo cheevo cheevio chee:
O where, what can thát be?
Weedio-weedio: there again!
So tiny a trickle of sóng-strain;
And all round not to be found
For brier, bough, furrow, or gréen ground
Before or behind or far or at hand

---

[113]See note to No. 62.

[114]Draft on one sheet of small notepaper in H. Fragments in some disorder: the arrange-ment of them in the text satisfies me. The word *sheath* is printed for *sheaf* of MS., and *sheaf* recurs in corrections. Dating of July 5, '76. [Note by R. Bridges.]

Either left either right
Anywhere in the súnlight.
Well, after all! Ah but hark—
"I am the little wóodlark.

        . . . .

To-day the sky is two and two
With white strokes and strains of the blue

        . . . .

Round a ring, around a ring
And while I sail (must listen) I sing

        . . . .

The skylark is my cousin and he
Is known to men more than me

        . . . .

...when the cry within
Says Go on then I go on
Till the longing is less and the good gone

But down drop, if it says Stop,
To the all-a-leaf of the tréetop
And after that off the bough

        . . . .

I ám so véry, O só very glad
That I dó thínk there is not to be had...

        . , ...

The blue wheat-acre is underneath
And the braided ear breaks out of the sheath,
The ear in milk, lush the sash,
And crush-silk poppies aflash,
The blood-gush blade-gash
Flame-rash rudred
Bud shelling or broad-shed
Tatter-tassel-tangled and dingle-a-dangled
Dandy-hung dainty head.

        . . . .

And down…the furrow dry
Sunspurge and oxeye
And laced-leaved lovely
Foam-tuft fumitory

. . . .

Through the velvety wind V-winged
To the nest's nook I balance and buoy
With a sweet joy of a sweet joy,
Sweet, of a sweet, of a sweet joy
Of a sweet—a sweet—sweet—joy."

65.[115]
Moonrise

Awoke in the Midsummer not to call night, |
   in the white and the walk of the morning:
The moon, dwindled and thinned to the fringe |
   of a finger-nail held to the candle,
Or paring of paradisaïcal fruit, |
   lovely in waning but lustreless,
Stepped from the stool, drew back from the barrow, |
   of dark Maenefa the mountain;
A cusp still clasped him, a fluke yet fanged him, |
   entangled him, not quit utterly.
This was the prized, the desirable sight, |
   unsought, presented so easily,
Parted me leaf and leaf, divided me, |
   eyelid and eyelid of slumber.

---

[115]"June 19, 1876." H. Note at foot shows intention to rewrite with one stress more
in the second half of each line, and the first is thus rewritten "in the white of the
dusk, in the walk of the morning." [Note by R. Bridges.]

66.[116]
"Repeat that, repeat"

Repeat that, repeat,
Cuckoo, bird, and open ear wells, heart-springs,
   delightfully sweet,
With a ballad, with a ballad, a rebound
Off trundled timber and scoops of the hillside ground,
   hollow hollow hollow ground:
The whole landscape flushes on a sudden at a sound.

[116]From a scrap in H without date or title. [Note by R. Bridges.]

67.[117]
On a piece of music

How all's to one thing wrought!

Facsimile **a**

---

[117]It being impossible to satisfy myself I give this MS. in facsimile as an example, a
and b. [Note by R. Bridges.]

Facsimile **b**

68.[118]
"The child is father to the man"

"The child is father to the man."
How can he be? The words are wild.
Suck any sense from that who can:
"The child is father to the man."
No; what the poet did write ran,
"The man is father to the child."
"The child is father to the man!"
How *can* he be? The words are wild.

69.[119]
"The shepherd's brow, fronting
forked lightning, owns"

The shepherd's brow, fronting forked lightning, owns
The horror and the havoc and the glory
Of it. Angels fall, they are towers, from heaven—a story
Of just, majestical, and giant groans.
But man—we, scaffold of score brittle bones;
Who breathe, from groundlong babyhood to hoary
Age gasp; whose breath is our *memento mori*—
What bass is *our* viol for tragic tones?
He! Hand to mouth he lives, and voids with shame;
And, blazoned in however bold the name,
Man Jack the man is, just; his mate a hussy.
And I that die these deaths, that feed this flame,
That…in smooth spoons spy life's masque mirrored: tame
My tempests there, my fire and fever fussy.

---

[118]From a newspaper cutting with another very poor comic triolet sent me by
G. M. H. They are signed "Bran." His comic attempts were not generally so
successful as this is. [Note by R. Bridges.]

[119]In H. Various consecutive full drafts on the same sheet as 51, and date April 3,
'89. The text is what seems to be the latest draft: it has no corrections. Thus its
date is between 50 and 51. It might be argued that this sonnet has the same right
to be recognised as a finished poem with the sonnets 44–47, but those had several
years' recognition whereas this must have been thrown off one day in a cynical
mood, which he could not have wished permanently to intrude among his last
serious poems. [Note by R..Bridges.]

70.[120]
To his Watch

Mortal my mate, bearing my rock-a-heart
Warm beat with cold beat company, shall I
Earlier or you fail at our force, and lie
The ruins of, rifled, once a world of art?
The telling time our task is; time's some part,
Not all, but we were framed to fail and die—
One spell and well that one. There, ah thereby
Is comfort's carol of all or woe's worst smart.

Field-flown, the departed day no morning brings
Saying "This was yours" with her, but new one, worse,
And then that last and shortest...

71.[121]
"Strike, churl; hurl, cheerless wind, then; heltering hail"

Strike, churl; hurl, cheerless wind, then; heltering hail
May's beauty massacre and wispèd wild clouds grow
Out on the giant air; tell Summer No,
Bid joy back, have at the harvest, keep Hope pale.

---

[120]On a sheet by itself; apparently a fair copy with corrections embodied in this text, except that the original 8th line, which is not deleted, is preferred to the alternative suggestion, *Is sweetest comfort's carol or worst woe's smart.* [Note by R. Bridges.]

[121]H, on same page with a draft of part of No. 45.—l. 4, *Have at* is a correction for *aim at.*—This scrap is some evidence for the earlier dating of the four sonnets. [Note by R. Bridges.]

72.[122]
Epithalamion

Hark, hearer, hear what I do; lend a thought now, make believe
We are leafwhelmed somewhere with the hood
Of some branchy bunchy bushybowered wood,
Southern dene or Lancashire clough or Devon cleave,
That leans along the loins of hills, where a candycoloured,
    where a gluegold-brown
Marbled river, boisterously beautiful, between
Roots and rocks is danced and dandled, all in froth
    and waterblowballs, down.
We are there, when we hear a shout
That the hanging honeysuck, the dogeared hazels in the cover
Makes dither, makes hover
And the riot of a rout
Of, it must be, boys from the town
Bathing: it is summer's sovereign good.
By there comes a listless stranger: beckoned by the noise
He drops towards the river: unseen
Sees the bevy of them, how the boys
With dare and with downdolphinry and bellbright bodies
    huddling out,
Are earthworld, airworld, waterworld thorough hurled,
    all by turn and turn about.
This garland of their gambols flashes in his breast
Into such a sudden zest
Of summertime joys
That he hies to a pool neighbouring; sees it is the best
There; sweetest, freshest, shadowiest;
Fairyland; silk-beech, scrolled ash, packed sycamore,
    wild wychelm, hornbeam fretty overstood
By. Rafts and rafts of flake-leaves light, dealt so,
    painted on the air,

---

[122]Four sides of pencilled rough sketches, and five sides of quarto first draft, on
"Royal University of Ireland" candidates paper, as if G. M. H. had written it
while supervising an examination. Fragments in disorder with erasures and corrections; undated. H.—The text, which omits only two disconnected lines, is
my arrangement of the fragments, and embodies the latest corrections. It was
to have been an Ode on the occasion of his brother's marriage, which fixes the
date as 1888. It is mentioned in a letter of May 25, whence the title comes.—I
have printed *dene* for *dean* (in two places). In l. 9 of poem *cover=covert,* which
should be in text, as G. M. H. never spelt phonetically.— l. 11, *of* may be *at,* MS.
uncertain.— l. 38, *shoots* is, I think, a noun. [Note by R. Bridges.]

Hang as still as hawk or hawkmoth, as the stars or
   as the angels there,
Like the thing that never knew the earth, never off roots
Rose. Here he feasts: lovely all is! No more: off with—
   down he dings
His bleachèd both and woolwoven wear:
Careless these in coloured wisp
All lie tumbled-to; then with loop-locks
Forward falling, forehead frowning, lips crisp
Over finger-teasing task, his twiny boots
Fast he opens, last he offwrings
Till walk the world he can with bare his feet
And come where lies a coffer, burly all of blocks
Built of chancequarrièd, selfquainèd, hoar-huskèd rocks
And the water warbles over into, filleted with glassy grassy
   quicksilvery shivès and shoots
And with heavenfallen freshness down from moorland
   still brims,
Dark or daylight on and on. Here he will then,
   here he will the fleet
Flinty kindcold element let break across his limbs
Long. Where we leave him, froliclavish while
   he looks about him, laughs, swims.

Enough now; since the sacred matter that I mean
I should be wronging longer leaving it to float
Upon this only gambolling and echoing-of-earth note—
What is...the delightful dene?
Wedlock. What the water? Spousal love.

       . . . .

Father, mother, brothers, sisters, friends
Into fairy trees, wild flowers, wood ferns
Rankèd round the bower

       . . . .

73.[123]
"Thee, God, I come from, to thee go"

Thee, God, I come from, to thee go,
All day long I like fountain flow
From thy hand out, swayed about
Mote-like in thy mighty glow.

What I know of thee I bless,
As acknowledging thy stress
On my being and as seeing
Something of thy holiness.

Once I turned from thee and hid,
Bound on what thou hadst forbid;
Sow the wind I would; I sinned:
I repent of what I did.

Bad I am, but yet thy child.
Father, be thou reconciled.
Spare thou me, since I see
With thy might that thou art mild.

I have life before me still
And thy purpose to fulfill;
Yea a debt to pay thee yet:
Help me, sir, and so I will.

But thou bidst, and just thou art,
Me shew mercy from my heart
Towards my brother, every other
Man my mate and counterpart.

. . . .

---

[123]Unfinished draft in H. Undated, probably '85, on same sheet with first draft of
No. 38.—l. 2, *day long*. MS. as two words with accent on *day*.—l. 17, above the
words *before me* the words *left with me* are written as alternative, but text is not
deleted. All the rest of this hymn is without question. In l. 19, *Yea* is right. After
the verses printed in text there is some versified *credo* intended to form part of
the complete poem; thus:
　Jesus Christ sacrificed
　On the cross....
　Moulded, he, in maiden's womb,
　Lived and died and from the tomb
　Rose in power and is our
　　Judge that comes to deal our doom.
[Note by R. Bridges.]

74.[124]
"To him who ever thought with love of me"

> To him who ever thought with love of me
> Or ever did for my sake some good deed
> I will appear, looking such charity
> And kind compassion, at his life's last need
> That he will out of hand and heartily
> Repent he sinned and all his sins be freed.

---

[124]Text is an underlined version among working drafts in H.—line 6, *freed* = got rid of, banished. This sense of the word is obsolete; it occurs twice in Shakespeare, cp. *Cymb.* III. vi. 79, "He wrings at some distress…would I could free 't!" [Note by R. Bridges.]

Alphabetical List of Titles and First Lines

Titles are given, in italics, only when distinct from the first lines.

~